Br

Bruce Lee

Bruce Lee

Simon Kenny

www.pocketessentials.com

This edition published in 2009 by Pocket Essentials
PO Box 394, Harpenden, Herts, AL5 1XJ

www.pocketessentials.com

A CIP catalogue record for this book is available from the British Library.

ISBN 978-1-84243-287-7

1 2 4 6 8 10 9 7 5 3

Typeset by Avocet Typeset, Chilton, Aylesbury, Bucks
Printed and bound in Great Britain by Cox & Wyman, Reading

Dedicated to the memory of Bruce Lee – a man of great determination.
If it were not for Bruce Lee then my life certainly would not be what it is.

This book is an introduction to Bruce Lee and in no way does it tell the complete story of Bruce Lee the man, the martial artist, the philosopher and the actor. My aim is that it will appeal to everybody – not just the newer fans of Bruce Lee, but the older ones too. I would be glad to hear any comments on the book; they can be emailed to me at sbkenny@hotmail.com.

Contents

Foreword

I first sat down to write the Pocket Essentials guide to Bruce Lee almost a decade ago in the year 2000. It was first published in 2001. At the time, Bruce Lee was as popular with mainstream audiences as he had been in the 1980s and 1990s. Today, his popularity is as strong as it has ever been.

As I write, there are numerous Bruce Lee projects on the horizon. There is a new Chinese mini-series based on his life. There are various books being written or about to be published and the final preparations are being made for the Bruce Lee exhibition to be held in conjunction with the UK's annual martial arts event SENI at the Excel Centre, London. Guests at the event include Bruce Lee's widow, Linda Lee Cadwell, his daughter Shannon Lee Keasler, plus appearances from Bruce's students and co-stars.

It would seem that the legend of 'the Little Dragon' continues to grow, almost 35 years since his passing. But what is it that makes Bruce Lee so popular after all these years?

It is number of things really. Bruce Lee appeals to a wide variety of people from all walks of life. He appeals to martial artists because of his amazing martial arts skills and incomparable work ethic. He is a role model for body-builders who admire his ripped physique. He is revered by action film fans for his outstanding choreography and realistic fight scenes. He is admired by thinkers and philosophers for his writings. He is respected by people regardless of creed or ethnic background.

It would be easy to pigeon-hole Bruce Lee as 'that Kung Fu guy', but he was so much more than a Kung Fu guy and evidence of that can still be seen.

Bruce Lee was unique. It would be unfair to say that no martial artist has ever attained the skill of Bruce Lee, or that no action film star could better Bruce Lee, because both statements are untrue. What sets Bruce Lee apart from everybody else was his ability to attain perfection in all that he chose to do, not just one field but many.

For a world-class body-builder to build a ripped physique requires him to live and breathe body-building; the same can be said for a world-class martial artist. Bruce Lee reached his peak in both fields on top of building a successful film career as an actor, producer, director and choreographer. He composed hundreds of pages of written documents, screenplays, poems, philosophical musings, books and magazine articles. He successfully managed a string of martial arts schools and coached world-champion fighters. And he still found time to be a loving husband and father, a full-time job in itself.

He achieved all of this by the age of 32.

Bruce Lee was in this world three years fewer than

he has now been out of it, but it is as if he never left. His legacy is strong to this day and I don't see it being forgotten any time soon.

Bruce Lee 1940–1973: may his spirit continue to guide.

Simon Kenny, March 2008

Introduction

Perhaps the greatest misconception about Bruce Lee was the suggestion that he was not a real martial artist, but a movie star masquerading as one, using camera tricks and favourable angles to make him look like a warrior on screen. The truth of the matter is that Bruce Lee was a martial artist first and a movie star second. Having studied martial arts from the age of 13 and philosophy at the University of Washington, Bruce Lee would choose to convey his art and philosophy through the medium of film.

The majority of the fighting that can be seen in Bruce Lee's films is a far cry from the martial arts he would use in real life. Bruce's art of Jeet Kune Do is a scientific method of streetfighting and there would be no chance of Bruce ever kicking somebody in the head in a street encounter – it just wouldn't be practical. In fact, it would be dangerous to even attempt it. One mistake and he would either find himself on his butt or the opponent grabbing hold of his leg and punishing him. But for the movies it is this type of glorified stage fighting that the audience wants to see. I would suggest that the majority of people who watch Bruce Lee's movies do so initially for the incredible fight scenes, but there is so much more to the films than the action.

Bruce Lee had a dynamic screen presence that has yet to be matched in martial arts films; he wouldn't need to say a word for the audience to know exactly what he was feeling at any particular moment in a film. Martial arts film stars of today rarely express any kind of emotion. Jackie Chan and Jet Li are perhaps the only exceptions, but even Jackie rarely demonstrates his acting ability, preferring to show the comedic element in his films. One good example of Jackie Chan's serious side can be seen in the film *Crime Story* (1993), but although Jackie puts in a great performance he still lacks the sheer magnetism of Bruce Lee. Something that people often fail to realise is that it is not what an actor says that makes you remember the performance, it is what he does. Think of the last film you went to see at the cinema, now try to remember the dialogue. You will no doubt remember one or two lines but not the complete script. However, you could tell the whole story to a third party by describing camera angles, facial expressions, and so on. Perhaps with his heavily accented dialogue Bruce did not come across as a convincing actor, but with his facial expressions he was incomparable. The four films that Bruce Lee completed did not have the most complex of stories, but with each movie Bruce tried to convey an underlying message or theme to the audience.

Upon his arrival in America in 1959, Bruce was faced with racial barriers that upset him a great deal, but rather than get angry or bitter he decided that he would do something about it and show America and the world something of the true Oriental. When producer William Dozier first signed Bruce for the *Green Hornet* television show, Bruce made it clear that he was not going to play the stereotypical house-boy role that had all too often been shown in Hollywood. As Bruce said, 'I told William Dozier, "Look, if you sign me up with all that pigtail and hopping around jazz, forget it." In the past, the typical casting has been that kind of stereotype. Like with the American Indian. You never see a human-being Indian on television.' Dozier respected Bruce's wishes and let him play the role of Kato as he wanted to. However, a few years later Bruce was again faced with racism in Hollywood, only this time it cost him the lead role in the television series *The Warrior*, later renamed *Kung Fu*. Legend has it that the reason Lee was rejected for this role was because he looked too Oriental to play an Oriental and the television company thought that the American audience would have a hard time accepting a Chinese man in a lead role. Lee commented, 'I have already made up my mind that in the United States, something about the Oriental – I mean the true Oriental – should be shown. I mean it has always been the same thing; the pigtail and the bouncing around saying "chop-chop" with the eyes slanted and all that. And that's very, very out of date. But the question as to how an American audience would react to an Oriental lead in a TV series was discussed and that is why my involvement in the series is probably not going to come off. Unfortunately such things as racism do exist in this world, you see. Like, in certain parts of the country, right? They think that, businesswise, it's a risk and I don't blame them. I mean, in the same way, it's like in Hong Kong; if a foreigner came here to become a star, if I were the man with the money, I probably would have my own worries about whether or not the public acceptance would be there.'

However, Bruce refused to let it make him cynical, and in all of his films he aimed to use actors of various races to get across the message that people were the same regardless of colour, religion or belief. In his first film, *The Big Boss*, Bruce used Thai extras; for *Fist of Fury* he used Japanese and Russians. In *Way of the Dragon* there were Italians, Americans, Japanese and Koreans. In *Enter the Dragon*, there were Americans, Afro-Caribbeans, Australians and Japanese; in *Game of Death* he used Filipinos, Koreans, Japanese, Australians, Taiwanese and Americans. People were people to Bruce and it didn't matter where they were from. True, he always defeated these guys and demonstrated that his art was superior, but he was the star after all.

Perhaps Bruce's biggest message against racism came in the film *Fist of Fury*. Throughout the film Bruce is faced with racism from the Japanese who claim that the Chinese are the 'sick men of Asia' and that the Japanese are the more powerful race. Bruce defeats the entire Japanese Karate school with his superior fighting skills – a blend of arts from various regions – thus demonstrating that it is not the origin of the art that is superior but the individual and, more importantly, the individual's morality.

Bruce also wanted to spread his philosophy on

martial arts and in each of his films he gives lessons on combat and philosophy. (The 'Underlying Theme' section in the film reviews gives a more detailed explanation of the combative lessons.)

Perhaps the performance that gives him the best opportunity to demonstrate his skills and philosophy as Bruce Lee the martial artist as opposed to Bruce Lee the actor is one that has very rarely been seen by a lot of fans: the television series *Longstreet*. Although Bruce wasn't the star of *Longstreet*, it was his character Li Tsung that proved the most popular with audiences all across America, evident through the amount of fanmail Bruce received compared to that of the star of the show, James Franciscus. Screenwriter Sterling Silliphant, who was a private student of Lee's, wrote the episode 'The Way of the Intercepting Fist' especially for his friend, but Lee's input is obvious. In this episode, Li Tsung teaches Mike Longstreet the basics of Jeet Kune Do and these scenes were based on Silliphant's real-life experiences whilst studying under Bruce. *Longstreet* is the only screen appearance Bruce made in which he demonstrates Jeet Kune Do – the way he would fight for real, not for the movies. He also wrote a lot of his own dialogue for the show, which may have been a little too deep for Western ears. Bruce's performance in *Longstreet* was very convincing and he demonstrated that he could play serious roles with ease.

It is difficult to comment on Bruce Lee the director as he only completed one film at the helm, *Way of the Dragon*. As well as being the producer, fight choreographer, scriptwriter and lead actor on this film, Bruce took over as director. The film was initially made purely for the Asian market so the storyline is quite simple, due to the fact that in the 1970s Asians tended to prefer their films that way. Also, there is a lot of Chinese humour in the film which Western audiences may struggle to find amusing. *Way of the Dragon*, however, was a landmark in Hong Kong cinema, being the first film ever to have location shots in a foreign country. These days, it is not unusual for Jackie Chan to shoot in two or three countries for one movie and have multiple roles in the production, but in 1971 for Bruce Lee to take a film crew to Rome and to take so many roles in the production process was an astonishing accomplishment.

In 1972 Bruce began work on what would have been his crowning glory, *Game of Death*, a multi-level film that he was to direct. Sadly, he only completed one-third of the film before his untimely death. Bruce's idea of a multi-level film was one that could be viewed on the surface level as a great action movie, but if you looked deeper you would find a much more meaningful film filled with philosophical insight into the combative arts. The scenes that Bruce did manage to complete were a montage of fight sequences that display his unequalled fight choreography. From his very first Hong Kong-produced picture, *The Big Boss*, to his very last, there is one element that just cannot be matched, his unique ability to choreograph realistic fight scenes. With *The Big Boss* and *Fist of Fury* the fight choreography credit goes to Han Ying Chieh and, while it is true that Han did choreograph some of the action, it was only for the

scenes that didn't directly involve Bruce – Bruce choreographed all his own fight scenes. The fact that Han
Ying Chieh was credited was merely a gesture of respect
from Bruce to the more senior Han. If you look at any
of the fight scenes involving Bruce and compare them
to the fight scenes he isn't in, the difference is evident.
Whereas Han's choreography was typical of the martial
arts genre of the 1960s and 1970s, using traditional
Kung Fu moves, Bruce's choreography was way ahead
of anything anybody had ever seen before – quick,
powerful kicks and punches with barely an edit. In fact,
in my opinion his choreography is still ahead of many of
today's top exponents. There are currently many
fantastic fight choreographers in the Hong Kong film
industry, such as Jackie Chan, Samo Hung, Yuen Biao,
Donnie Yen, Yuen Woo Ping, but they rely on the ability
to edit, which Bruce rarely did. He would invariably use
a wide-angle shot and film the whole sequence in one
take, proving that he really was able to do what was
shown on the screen. No camera tricks and no (or very
few) edits. For the final duel with Chuck Norris in *Way
of the Dragon*, Bruce wrote out every detail of the action,
taking up one-third of the script and making it the most
realistic and thrilling fight scene ever captured on
celluloid.

So for those of you who think that Bruce Lee was
just a martial artist I would implore you to take a closer
look. Bruce Lee was an actor, a screenwriter, a director,
a choreographer, a philosopher, a poet, a husband and a
father. Most importantly, Bruce Lee was a human
being, and one with no limitations.

Early Life

Birth of the Little Dragon

During late 1940, Li Hoi Chuen and his heavily pregnant wife Grace Lee were touring the United States with the Cantonese Opera troupe, of which Hoi Chuen was a veteran performer. He was a famous actor in his native Hong Kong, but had decided to go to America with the troupe to perform in a stage play. On the 27 November Grace gave birth to her fourth child, Bruce Jun Fan Lee, at San Francisco's Jackson Street hospital in Chinatown. Bruce was born between 6:00 am and 8:00 am, during the Hour of the Dragon, in what was also the Year of the Dragon. Because Bruce was born in the USA he automatically assumed American citizenship, which would allow him in later life to live legally in the USA. When he was only three months old he got his first on-screen experience in the American-produced *Golden Gate Girl*. Shortly after the young baby's debut in early 1941, the family headed back to Hong Kong where Hoi Chuen continued his work in the film industry.

Child Actor

Before Bruce Lee became a famous actor in adulthood, he was a big star as a child actor in Hong Kong. When Bruce was around five years old he started visiting his father on the sets of his films. He was mesmerised; he would stand off-camera and mimic his father on set. A director noticed Bruce on the set and was so impressed by the youngster's talents that he offered him a part in the film, an offer which Bruce and his father happily accepted. This would be the start of a very successful film career that would see Bruce appear in more than 20 films over the next 11 or so years, often typecast as a young street urchin. The audiences went wild for Bruce Lee and soon gave him the nickname 'Lee Siu Loong' – 'Lee the Little Dragon' – a name that would stick with him throughout his life. Fans of Bruce Lee still call him 'the Little Dragon' to this day.

The films were a true reflection of Bruce's real-life childhood in Hong Kong. Most of them have probably been lost by now – the Hong Kong film industry has never been big on archiving movies. To them, making movies is a consumable business like any other and once a film has had its run at the cinema, it is generally discarded. An old video release back in the early 1980s called *The Real Bruce Lee* is the best source of clips from some of these movies. Below is a list of some of the films Bruce Lee made as a child in Hong Kong. (Some of the English titles may be slightly different from what you may have seen elsewhere due to differences in translation.)

1941 *Golden Gate Girl*
1946 *The Birth of Mankind*
1950 *Kid Cheung*
1951 *The Kid*
1951 *Infancy*
1953 *The Guiding Light*
1953 *In the Face of Demolition*
1953 *It's Father's Fault*
1953 *A Mother's Tears*
1953 *Myriad Homes*
1955 *Love*
1955 *An Orphan's Tragedy*
1955 *The Faithful Wife*
1955 *Orphan's Song*
1955 *We Owe It to Our Children*
1956 *Wise Guys Fool Around*
1956 *Too Late for Divorce*
1957 *The Thunderstorm*
1957 *Darling Girl*
1957 *The Orphan*

The Rebellious Teen

As a child, Bruce Lee was very active, so much so that his family nicknamed him 'Mo Si Tung' ('Never Sits Still'). At age 13 he was beaten up by a bully and vowed it would never happen again. So, to defend himself and to channel his bottled-up energy, he began studying Wing Chun Kung Fu under the instruction of the legendary Grandmaster Yip Man. Before long, Bruce became one of Master Yip's best pupils, perhaps because of his eagerness to learn, or perhaps because quite often Bruce was the only student in the class. This wasn't because Master Yip had a shortage of students, but because Bruce would often turn up to class early and wait outside for all the other students to show up. He would then tell them that the class had been cancelled because Master Yip was unwell or out of town and so get the benefit of a full session with the Master to himself!

By the time Bruce was 14 years old he had become involved with a street gang called 'the Junction Street 8 Tigers'. The Tigers were a new gang formed by the kids who lived in the Junction Street district of Kowloon. They had decided to stand up for justice, help the weak and fight the bullies. As a member of the gang Bruce would often find himself in trouble with the police for fighting whilst trying out the Kung Fu that he had learned from Yip Man. With his good friend and senior Kung Fu brother, William Cheung, Bruce would often challenge fighters from other Kung Fu schools. The fights usually took place on the rooftops high above the bustling Kowloon City. Cheung recalls some of these fights in the book *Mystery of Bruce Lee* (a deleted publication by the Bruce Lee JKD club, Hong Kong, 1980). Not all of the fights would be fair one-on-one tests of Kung Fu, however. Sometimes they would get so far out of hand that literally dozens of people would be brawling with sticks and knives.

At about the same time, Bruce began taking cha-cha lessons mainly as a way to meet girls, but soon found that he could incorporate the footwork into his Wing

Chun training. Even at such a young age, Bruce was integrating outside influences into his martial arts training. He went on to become so good at cha-cha dancing that in 1958 he won the Crown Colony cha-cha championships.

After a couple of years' training with Yip Man, some of the other students found out that Bruce's mother had German ancestry. They were not happy that Master Yip was teaching Wing Chun to somebody with Western blood and asked him to expel Bruce from the class. Master Yip refused, but after some serious consideration Bruce decided that he would leave of his own accord. He continued his training under the instruction of two of Master Yip's senior students, Wong Shun Leung and William Cheung. Every weekend he travelled to the farm where William lived in the New Territories of Hong Kong and work out.

Return to America

In 1958, Bruce's temporary citizenship for the United States was coming to an end and he would have to travel back to America if he wished to obtain full citizenship. His parents were tired of Bruce getting into trouble with the police and feared for his safety. He had recently been expelled from high school, plus had a price on his head from many local gangs; it was decided therefore that it would be in his best interests to leave Hong Kong for America. In March 1959, with a little over $100 in his pocket, Bruce boarded a liner with a friend of his father and set off on a three-week voyage for San Francisco. The ship's crew let Bruce spend most of his evening in first class in return for teaching the first-class passengers how to cha-cha, but when the evening's festivities ended Bruce would return back down to steerage where he would sleep until the next day. Bruce and his father's friend didn't really see eye-to-eye on the voyage so when they arrived in America, they went their separate ways. The father's friend stayed in San Francisco, whilst Bruce made his way to Seattle and stayed with another of his father's friends, Ruby Chow. Ruby had a Chinese restaurant in Seattle and Bruce took a room upstairs in return for waiting tables in the restaurant. Whilst working, Bruce enrolled at Edison Technical College, where his favourite subjects were philosophy and history. He already had a deep interest in Chinese philosophy from his martial arts background. After studying diligently Bruce gained his high-school diploma.

In 1961 Bruce entered the University of Washington, majoring in Philosophy. It was here that Bruce met Linda Emery whilst he was giving a lecture at Garfield High School. It was love at first sight for Linda; she compared Bruce to the handsome young Puerto Rican actor George Chakiris who played Bernardo in *West Side Story*. Linda had a Chinese girlfriend at Garfield High School and before long she found herself spending many an evening in Chinatown taking Kung Fu classes with Bruce Lee, who would be teaching a small group of people in a local parking lot. After the lesson the class would make its way to a nearby Chinese restaurant, or go to the cinema to watch a Japanese samurai film.

When Bruce opened his first real Kung Fu school near the university campus, Linda became a regular student. Bruce moved out of Ruby Chow's restaurant and lived behind his classroom in a room that didn't even have a window, just a hole where the glass should be. However, Bruce was happy to be out of Chow's and completely independent.

Bruce and Linda's friendship grew, until one day out of the blue he asked her if she would like to go to the Space Needle with him. Linda thought that Bruce meant with the rest of the class, but when he said just her she couldn't believe her luck. It would be the start of a strong and loving relationship.

After a short trip to Hong Kong with one of his students, Doug Palmer, Bruce opened a second Kung Fu school in Oakland, California, where he also set up home. In August 1964, Bruce and Linda were married. Taky Kimura, one of Bruce's senior students, was his best man. Linda's parents were unaware of the fact that their daughter was seeing an Oriental – the first they knew of it was when Bruce and Linda announced their marriage. Linda's parents only wanted the best for their daughter and were worried that marriage to someone of another race would complicate her life, but as Linda saw it, Bruce was a human being and that was all – there were no divisions of colour, creed or race.

Discovering a Star

Bruce's Kung Fu schools were doing great business and proved very popular with a lot of Westerners. In 1964 he was invited to give a display of his Kung Fu at the Long Beach International Karate Championships hosted by Ed Parker, the Grandfather of American Kenpo karate. Bruce gave various demonstrations of his Kung Fu and had the audience gasping at his demonstration of the one-inch punch. He would stand with his fist an inch from an opponent's chest and punch with such devastating power that it would knock the person back five or six feet.

Also at the tournament that day was Dan Inosanto, the Filipino martial arts expert, who was competing in the black belt category. After the tournament had ended Bruce and Dan were introduced to one another and they immediately struck up a friendship. From that day on, Bruce and Dan would spend many hours together every week training in what Dan described as a devastatingly improved version of Wing Chun. But Dan was not only Bruce's student, he was also Bruce's teacher and introduced him to Filipino weapons like the nunchaku, which Bruce would use to great effect in his films. Dan also introduced Bruce to the Filipino empty hand arts.

Bruce's schools continued to grow and his name was spreading far and wide. However, the Chinese fraternity in California didn't like the fact that Bruce was showing his martial art to foreigners and made their feelings known. It is widely believed that Bruce received many challenges and threats from some of the Chinese Masters of Kung Fu in California, the most famous being the challenge from Wong Jack Man. Wong Jack Man was a Kung Fu teacher who had recently arrived in America from Hong Kong. He believed that Kung Fu was a Chinese art that should only be taught to Chinese people. Seeking to make a name for himself in America, Wong Jack Man issued a written challenge to Bruce, with the loser having to close his school. A time and place were scheduled for the challenge and Wong, along with several of his students, arrived with a list of rules and regulations. However, Bruce insisted that it should be an all-out, no-holds-barred fight; it was about honour and winning the right to teach whom he wished. Unable to back down in front of his students, Wong reluctantly agreed. The fight was nothing like the kind of fighting Bruce would become famous for in his films; this was reality and it was fast and messy. A few exchanges of blows were made and then Bruce attacked with a Wing Chun 'straight blast' – a continuous barrage of straight punches to the head. Wong Jack Man turned his back under the pressure and began fleeing from Bruce, who followed him around the gym punching at the back of his head. The result was Bruce would not close his school and would continue to teach his art to Westerners. But rather than be happy with his victory, Bruce was deeply annoyed. The fight had lasted a full three minutes and by the end of it he was exhausted. The fight should have lasted mere seconds but he couldn't land a finishing blow. It was time to rethink his art and also to reassess his physical conditioning.

However, Bruce's life was about to take a step in another direction, with his acting talents being called to the fore once more. One of the spectators at the Long Beach tournament had been Jay Sebring, a student of Ed Parker. Sebring had a hair salon in Beverly Hills, where one of his clients was William Dozier, the producer of the *Batman* television series. During one of his appointments Dozier mentioned to Sebring that he was looking for an Oriental to cast in a new series he was developing called *Number One Son*, a spin-off from the Charlie Chan movies. Sebring immediately recalled Bruce's demonstration at the Long Beach tournament and suggested Dozier should get in touch with him.

By now Bruce and Linda had moved into James

Yimm Lee's house in Oakland after James' wife had passed away. It was a real family affair with Bruce, Linda, James and James' two children. On 1 February 1965, Linda gave birth to their first child, Brandon Bruce Lee; three days later Bruce attended a screen test for *Number One Son* at the Warner Brothers film studio. As the cameras rolled Bruce introduced himself and answered questions about his film career in Hong Kong and about his martial art before giving a demonstration on a rather worried-looking stage extra. Bruce's demonstration was extremely impressive, but what was more impressive was the sheer screen presence that he had – the camera loved him.

Three weeks after the screen test Bruce's father passed away in Hong Kong and Bruce left the United States to attend the funeral. Linda did not go, but went instead to introduce her new son to her mother. Linda's mother had still not fully accepted the marriage and greeted Linda at the door with, 'How could you do this?'

When Bruce returned to Oakland, William Dozier called to say that the *Number One Son* series had been cancelled, but he had Bruce in mind for another role playing Kato, the Oriental sidekick to the Green Hornet, a comic book hero in the Batman vein. Bruce was elated, although he swore that he was offered the role because he was the only Oriental on the west coast who could pronounce the name of the Green Hornet's alter ego, Britt Reid. Bruce was paid the grand sum of $400 per episode, with 30 episodes planned for the first season. Now that he had a job, Bruce decided it was time that his family moved out of James Lee's house and in March 1966 they moved to a small apartment in Westwood.

The Green Hornet and Kato

The Green Hornet aired on 9 September 1966 and Bruce's Kung Fu caused a sensation among its younger viewers. They had never before seen this kind of fighting. Bruce became an instant star and was asked to attend dozens of personal appearances and promotional tours for the show, receiving up to $1,000 per appearance. *The Green Hornet* was about a newspaper magnate, Britt Reid (played by Van Williams), who at night would don a mask, trilby hat and green overcoat to fight crime with his trusty manservant, Kato. Each week, the Hornet, armed with his Hornet Sting gun and Kato with his hands and feet of fury would jump into their gadget-laden car, The Black Beauty, and set out on missions of justice.

The Green Hornet – Cast

Cast: Van Williams (Britt Reid/The Green Hornet), Bruce Lee (Kato), Wende Wagner (Lenore 'Casey' Case), Lloyd Gough (Mike Axford), Walter Brooke (District Attorney FP Scanlon)

Crew: William Dozier (Executive Producer), Billy May (Music), Al Hirt (Rimsky-Korsakov's theme, 'The

Flight of the Bumblebee'), Jack A Marta (Director of Photography)

1. 'The Silent Gun'
First Aired: 9 September 1966
Plot: The Green Hornet goes after a deadly silent gun that is responsible for a series of crimes.
Guest Stars: Lloyd Bochner (Dan Carley), Henry Evans (Renner), Kelly Jean Peters (Jackie), Ed McGrealy (Olsen), Max Kelvin (Stacey), L McGranary (Minister)

2. 'Give 'Em Enough Rope'
First Aired: 16 September 1966
Plot: The Green Hornet and Kato break a phoney accident ring.
Guest Stars: Diana Hyland (Claudia Bromley), Mort Mills (Alex Colony), Jerry Ayers (Pete), Joe Sirola (Charley), David Renard (Joe Sweek), Ken Strange (Big Bruiser)

3. 'Programmed for Death'
First Aired: 23 September 1966
Plot: The Green Hornet and his trusty aide Kato bring about the capture of a ring of phoney diamond merchants who are responsible for the death of one of Reid's reporters.
Guest Stars: Signe Hasso (Yolanda de Lukens), Richard Cutting (Frank Miller), Norman Leavitt (Walter Melvin), Pat Tidy (Charwoman), Barbara Babcock (Cathy Desmond), Gary Owens (Commentator)

4. 'Crime Wave'
First Aired: 30 September 1966
Plot: The Green Hornet cracks a computer crime wave that has implicated him as its leader.
Guest Stars: Peter Haskell (Abel Marcus), Sheilah Wells (Laura Spinner), Ron Burke (Joe), Gary Owens (Commentator), Denny Costello (Detective)

5. 'The Frog Is a Deadly Weapon'
First Aired: 7 October 1966
Plot: The Green Hornet uncovers a missing crook masquerading as a wealthy financier whom he has murdered.
Guest Stars: Victor Jory (Charles Delaclaire), Thordis Brandt (Nedra Vallen)

6. 'Eat, Drink and Be Dead'
First Aired: 14 October 1966
Plot: The crime-fighting duo uncover an illegal alcohol racket.
Guest Stars: Jason Evers (Henry Dirk), Harry Lauter (Brannigan), Eddie Ness (Crandall), Harry Fleer (Evans)

7. 'Beautiful Dreamer Part 1'
First Aired: 21 October 1966
Plot: The Green Hornet discovers that a well-known health-club owner is brainwashing his clients for criminal purposes.
Guest Stars: Geoffrey Horne (Peter Eden), Pamela Curran (Vanessa), Victoria George (Harriet), Barbara

Gates (Mary), Maurice Manson (Cavanaugh), Gary Owens (TV Announcer), Jean Marie (Dorothy)

8. 'Beautiful Dreamer Part 2'
First Aired: 28 October 1966
Plot: The Green Hornet traps the brainwashing health-club owner in his own subliminal suggestion gimmick.
Guest Stars: as Part 1

9. 'The Ray Is for Killing'
First Aired: 11 November 1966
Plot: The Green Hornet and Kato foil a million-dollar art heist.
Guest Stars: Grant Woods (Steve), Robert McQueeney (Richardson), Bill Baldin (Dr Karl Bendix), Mike Mahoney (Policeman), Jim Raymond (Driver)

10. 'The Praying Mantis'
First Aired: 18 November 1966
Plot: The crime-fighting duo take on a Master of Praying Mantis Kung Fu.
Guest Stars: Mako (Low Sing), Allen Jung (Wing Ho), Tom Drake (Duke Slate), Gary Owens (Announcer), Al Huang (Jimmy Kee), Dan Inosanto (Mako's Martial Arts double)

11. 'The Hunters and the Hunted'
First Aired: 25 November 1966

Plot: A club of big-game hunters make the Hornet their largest pray.
Guest Stars: Robert Strauss (Bud Crocker), Charles Bateman (Quentin Crane), Douglas Evans (LeLand Stone)

12. 'Deadline for Death'
First Aired: 2 December 1966
Plot: Mike Axford is on a murder charge and only the Hornet can prove his innocence.
Guest Stars: James Best (Yale Burton), Linda Day George (Ardis Ralston)

13. 'The Secret of Sally Bell'
First Aired: 9 December 1966
Plot: The Green Hornet and Kato smash a drug ring.
Guest Stars: Walter Kemmerling (Bert Selden), Beth Brickell (Dr Thomas), Dave Perna (Wolfe), Greg Benedict (Carlos), Jacques Denbeaux (Gus Wander)

14. 'Freeway to Death'
First Aired: 16 December 1966
Plot: The Green Hornet uncovers a construction company insurance racket.
Guest Stars: Jeffrey Hunter (Emmet Crown), David Fresco (Wiggens), John Hubbard (Giles), Reggie Parton (Spike)

15. 'May the Best Man Lose'
First Aired: 23 December 1966
Plot: The Green Hornet seeks out the assassin of the

District Attorney, risking his own identity in the process.

Guest Stars: Linden Chiles (Warren Ryland), Robert Hoy (Woody), Harold Gould (Calvin Ryland), Troy Melton (Pete)

16. 'Seek, Stalk and Destroy'
First Aired: 6 January 1967
Plot: Three Korean War veterans plot to spring their former commander, wrongfully accused of murder, from prison.
Guest Stars: Ralph Meeker (Earl Evans), Raymond St Jacques (Hollis Silver), Paul Carr (Eddie Carter), John Baer (Bradford Devlin)

17. 'Corpse of the Year Part 1'
First Aired: 13 January 1967
Plot: Britt Reid is startled by the attack on his *Daily Sentinel* by somebody pretending to be the Green Hornet.
Guest Stars: Joanne Dru (Sabrina), Cesare Danova (Felix Garth), Tom Simcox (Dan Scully), Celia Kaye (Melissa Neal)

18. 'Corpse of the Year Part 2'
First Aired: 20 January 1967
Plot: The Hornet's trap for an impostor pits Black Beauty against a twin Black Beauty.
Guest Stars: as Part 1

19. 'Bad Bet On 459-Silent'
First Aired: 3 February 1967
Plot: While exposing crooked cops, the Green Hornet is wounded by the police and nearly killed by Mike Axford.
Guest Stars: Richard Anderson (Phil Trager), Tony Epper (Nixie), Richard X Slattery (Steve Grant), Bill Couch (Carns), Percy Helton (Gus), Bill Hampton (Jess)

20. 'Ace in the Hole'
First Aired: 10 February 1967
Plot: By pitting one member against another, the Green Hornet smashes a dangerous criminal cartel.
Guest Stars: Bert Freed (Sgt. Bert Clark), Jason Wingreen (Doctor), Brian Avery (Jim Dixon)

21. 'Trouble for Prince Charming'
First Aired: 17 February 1967
Plot: The Green Hornet becomes involved in a plot to oust the young prince of a foreign power.
Guest Stars: Alberto Morin (Abu Bakr), Susan Flannery (Janet Prescott), James Lanphier (Sarajek), Edmund Hashim (Prince Rafil)

22. 'Alias "The Scarf"'
First Aired: 24 February 1967
Plot: In a wax museum caper, the Green Hornet and Kato trap a strangler who has been immortalised in wax.
Guest Stars: John Carradine (James Rancourt), Ian

Wolfe (Peter Wilman), Patricia Barry (Hazel Schmidt), Paul Gleason (Paul Garret)

23. 'Hornet, Save Thyself'
First Aired: 3 March 1967
Plot: A gun that seemingly shoots by itself almost puts Britt Reid in prison.
Guest Stars: Michael Strong (Dale Hyde), Marvin Brody (Eddie Rich)

24. 'Invasion from Outer Space Part 1'
First Aired: 10 March 1967
Plot: The Green Hornet attempts to stop a power-mad scientist from stealing a nuclear warhead.
Guest Stars: Linda Gaye Scott (Vama), Larry Mann (Dr Eric Mabouse), Christopher Dark (Martin), Arthur Batanides (Shugo), Denny Dobins (Colonel)

25. 'Invasion from Outer Space Part 2'
First Aired: 17 March 1967
Plot: The Green Hornet escapes certain death and tries to prevent the detonation of the H-bomb warhead.
Guest Stars: as Part 1

26. 'The Hornet and the Firefly'
First Aired: 24 March 1967
Plot: An arsonist seeks to destroy Mike Axford and the city's lifeline. Can the Green Hornet stop him?
Guest Stars: Gerald S O'Loughlin (Ben Wade), Russ Conway (Commissioner Dolan)

The Guest Star

Due to falling ratings, *The Green Hornet* was cancelled after only 26 episodes. However, the duo did make one more appearance, as guest stars in *Batman*. At first, the Hornet and Kato battle Batman and Robin, then they later team up to fight crime together. As the shows both had big fan bases, the producers agreed to let the characters only fight to a draw so as not to upset anybody. On the day of filming the fight scene, the Hornet would be fighting Batman and Kato would be fighting Robin. Burt Ward, who played Robin, is reported to have thought himself to be a pretty tough character who knew how to look after himself. It was rumoured that he had told certain people on the set that he would be able to take Bruce Lee in real life, word of which reached Bruce. Studio gossip then got back to Ward that Bruce was going to seriously damage him. When the cameras began rolling, Bruce's eyes burned into Ward and he truly looked like he was going to kill him; Ward was petrified. The scene went well with no serious injuries and after the camera had stopped rolling someone made a chicken sound aimed at Ward. The crew cracked up laughing. Bruce looked over at Burt Ward and said, 'It's a good job it ain't real life,' then he also burst into laughter.

Batman

Cast: Adam West (Batman), Burt Ward (Robin), Van Williams (the Green Hornet), Bruce Lee (Kato)

Episode: 'A Piece of the Action'
First Aired: 1 March 1967

Episode: 'Batman's Satisfaction'
First Aired: 2 March 1967

What Is Jeet Kune Do?

After *The Green Hornet* came off air Bruce Lee found himself once more without a regular job, so he went back to what he knew best, continuing to develop his martial art, both for himself and to teach it in order to earn some money. Bruce carried on working with Dan Inosanto and one day whilst out driving they got into a discussion about fencing. Bruce's elder brother, Peter, was a champion fencer and had been a representative for the Asian Games in 1956. The discussion continued and Bruce said that the most effective counter in fencing was the 'stop hit', a method by which you parry the opponent's attack while making your own attack in the same instant. Bruce remarked that his martial art had evolved into a similar principle and said to Dan that perhaps he should name his art, 'The Stop Hit Way'. Dan asked what the Chinese interpretation of that would be and Bruce replied, in Cantonese, 'Jeet Kune Do'.

Jeet Kune Do became Bruce Lee's personal expression of the martial arts specifically tailored to his own attributes and capabilities. Today, there are many proponents of Jeet Kune Do across the globe, teaching some of Bruce Lee's original concepts and ideas. But what many people fail to realise is that Jeet Kune Do is a personal development. What worked for Bruce Lee won't necessarily work for another person. This was his personal philosophy: one man's truth may not be the same as another's.

Bruce Lee began his martial arts training in 1953, studying Wing Chun Kung Fu under the famed Grandmaster Yip Man. He had had his first introduction into the martial arts from his father a couple of years before, when he was shown a Tai Chi form, but Yip Man was his first real instructor. Bruce also picked up forms and techniques from other types of Chinese Kung Fu, including Choy Li Fut, Northern Praying Mantis and Hung Gar styles, as well as techniques in fencing from his elder brother Peter. But Wing Chun was his core system and Bruce trained under Master Yip and two of his top students, William Cheung and Wong Shun Leung, for five or six years until he left Hong Kong for America.

Whilst in America, Bruce continued his Wing Chun training, but also began collecting books on various martial arts, including Karate, Praying Mantis Kung Fu, French Savate (Boxe Française), Judo, wrestling, Tae Kwon Do and Western and Thai Boxing.

Bruce also met some martial artists in America who would help shape the way he perceived the martial arts and introduce him to new methods and skills. Jhoon Rhee is today considered the Grandfather of American Tae Kwon Do. When he first met Bruce in 1964, Bruce was only using Wing Chun kicking techniques, which were generally kept below waist height. Jhoon Rhee introduced Bruce to the high kicking of Tae Kwon Do and also to the art of board-breaking. Although Bruce thought board-breaking was merely a stunt, he would often practise it because that was what people wanted to see at demonstrations. Bruce developed his kicking techniques and before long he was kicking at head height, using spinning kicks and flying kicks. However, these kicking techniques were only used in the movies. For real-life combat, Bruce would stick to the low-line kicks of Wing Chun, aiming for targets such as the shin, knee and groin.

In 1964 Bruce also met Filipino martial artist Dan Inosanto at the 1964 Long Beach International Karate Championships. Dan was a black belt in Kenpo Karate under Grandmaster Ed Parker. He had also studied Judo and the Filipino martial arts of stick and sword fighting with an uncle who was an Escrimador and later with such notable Escrimamen as Max Sarmiento, Regino Elustrismo, Gilbert Tenio, Angel Cabales and John Lacoste. Dan had been a top athlete at high school, competing in track and field events and, despite his size, was also a member of the football team. He would later introduce Bruce to some of the training equipment used in American football, such as the air shield, which Bruce adopted for practising his kicks. Dan would become Bruce's number one student and Bruce would pass on as much knowledge and skill as Dan could take onboard. But Dan also became Bruce's instructor, teaching him what he knew about the Filipino arts and also how to use the nunchaku, a weapon for which he would later become identified, and Escrima.

Bruce and Dan had a great friendship and today Dan Inosanto is considered the foremost authority and mantle holder of Jeet Kune Do. Dan was Bruce's main sparring partner and the two worked out as often as possible. It was Dan to whom Bruce turned after his encounter with Wong Jack Man in 1965 and told him that his art needed to be adapted because it wasn't as efficient as it should be. Dan recalled Bruce telling him, 'I chased him and like a fool, kept punching his head. My fists were already swelling from his hard head. Then, I did something I'd never done before; I just put my arm round his neck and knocked him on his ass. I kept whacking him as he lay on the floor, until he gave up. I was so tired I could hardly punch him.' It was after this encounter that Jeet Kune Do was really born and Bruce began to train for efficiency and economy of motion.

The name Jeet Kune Do was first coined in 1967, but Bruce eventually came to resent the fact that he had ever given his art a name because people tend to cling to it. When people attach a name to something it becomes gospel and static, which is against all that Jeet Kune Do stands for. Jeet Kune Do is about freedom, liberation, adaptability and evolution to use 'no way, as the way'.

Many people describe Jeet Kune Do as a style of fighting but it isn't a style at all, it is a process of continual growth and development. Bruce didn't believe in styles, such as a Japanese style of fighting or a Chinese way of fighting, because unless human beings have three arms or four legs there cannot be another form or way of fighting. There can only be one style of fighting but you can incorporate different methods, techniques and attributes into your art, such as footwork, timing, speed, spatial relationship and so on.

Bruce Lee trained with a lot of other martial artists, such as World Karate champions Joe Lewis, Bob Wall, Mike Stone and Chuck Norris. He trained in Judo and grappling under Gene Le Bell. He trained in Boxe Française, Western Boxing and Thai Boxing. He trained in wrestling with Larry Hartsell, who has sadly passed away since the first publication of this book, and he trained in fencing with his brother Peter. Although many of these martial artists were considered students of Bruce Lee, he probably learnt as much from them as they did from him. Jeet Kune Do is a blend of all these arts and more. Bruce believed that no art was superior to another, that every art is effective depending upon the circumstances. For example, a Thai round kick to the thigh is a devastating technique, but it is useless in a telephone box. Similarly, a Wing Chun straight blast is a very effective close-quarter technique, but when you and your opponent are five feet apart and your opponent is holding a six-foot stick it is not so efficient. A good Jeet Kune Do man should flow from one range to another without thinking. He should flow naturally in and out of each range, from kicking to punching to trapping to grappling. Bruce described Jeet Kune Do as: 'a smooth, rhythmic expression of smashing the guy before he hits you, with any method available'.

Bruce Lee's Philosophy

Bruce Lee's martial art of Jeet Kune Do was as much a way of thinking as it was a way of doing. Bruce studied philosophy at the University of Washington in the early 1960s and incorporated much of what he learnt into his daily life and Jeet Kune Do. Bruce read a lot of the works of Alan Watts and J Krishnamurti and was influenced by Buddhism, Taoism, Confucianism and many other religious and philosophical sources. From these he developed his own philosophy. Below are some examples of Bruce Lee's thoughts and quotes that relate to his martial arts studies and to his way of life. It is my hope that they will give you a small insight into Bruce Lee the Philosopher.

Man, the living creature, the creating individual is always more important than any established style.
Bruce Lee did not believe in styles or systems. He once said that unless there was another species of human being with more arms or legs than us, then we could not have another style of fighting. Jeet Kune Do is the style of no style, the way of no way. From the next couple of quotes we can perhaps understand a little more.

The truth is outside of all fixed patterns.
You can't organise truth; that is like trying to put a pound of water into wrapping paper and shaping it.

All types of knowledge ultimately mean self-knowledge.
Bruce had an enormous desire to learn. He believed

that the more we learn, the more we learn about ourselves.

Empty your mind; be formless, shapeless. Like water. Now you can put water into a cup and it becomes that cup. You put water into a bottle and it becomes the bottle. You put it into a teapot and it becomes the teapot. Now water can flow or it can crash. Be water, my friend.

One day after training with Yip Man, Bruce got pretty frustrated with his training and set out on a boat on his own. As he was lying in the boat he noticed a bird flying above and then observed its reflection in the water. A thought suddenly struck him and he punched out at the water, but the water just returned to its original state. He tried once more to damage the water but again it returned to its original form. He suddenly realised that no matter how hard he tried he could not damage the water. He also knew that water could penetrate the hardest rocks and granite and eventually over time bring down large mountains. If he could adapt himself to be like water he could flow with his opponent's every move; he could mould himself into any shape or form he desired. He would be soft and flowing until the point of attack; then he would be hard and crash like the greatest of waves.

Knowing is not enough, we must apply. Willing is not enough, we must do.

This quote speaks for itself – many a person has the knowledge and the desire, but lacks the ability to put it into action.

I don't want to be like 'As Confucius say', but under the sky, under the heavens there is but one family. It just so happens that people are different.

When Bruce married Linda racism was rife in America. Bruce did not see Linda as a Caucasian nor did she see Bruce as an Oriental. To Bruce, Linda was a woman and to Linda he was a man. This is how Bruce always saw people, as human beings. Nothing more. Nothing less.

A good martial artist does not become tense but ready. Not thinking yet not dreaming, ready for whatever may come. A martial artist has to take responsibility for himself and face the consequences of his own doing. To have no technique, there is no opponent, because the word 'I' does not exist. When the opponent expands, I contract, and when he contracts, I expand. And when there is an opportunity, 'I' do not hit, 'It' hits all by itself.

As I have already said, Bruce Lee did not believe in styles or fixed patterns. There are times when one technique will work and another won't. Circumstance is a prevalent factor in any encounter. When your mind is concentrating on techniques and what to do next in a fight, all awareness of the fight is lost. *To have no technique… the word 'I' does not exist.* This means that 'I' will not hit but when an opportunity presents itself 'It' hits all by itself. The mind is free from clutter and is only aware of being.

For further insight into the philosophy of Bruce Lee, I suggest you read the books published by the Bruce Lee Educational Foundation, edited by John Little. Some of them are listed in the reference section of this book.

More TV and Film Work

Further Guest Appearances

After Bruce's success on *The Green Hornet* he was approached by several individuals to open a chain of Kato Karate schools that would have made him a millionaire. Bruce declined because he saw it as prostituting an art that he had worked for years to develop. Instead, he opened his third Kung Fu school in College Street, Chinatown, where Dan Inosanto became his assistant instructor. This school was unlike the previous two he had opened because he would no longer accept beginners into his classes, only martial artists who were already accomplished in another art. Also, he would not charge his students, but opted instead to make his money by teaching martial arts to celebrities such as Steve McQueen, James Coburn, James Garner, Roman Polanski and Kareem Abdul Jabbar, charging up to $250 an hour. He would also make extra money by appearing in various television shows as a guest star. These appearances are listed below.

Ironside

Episode: 'Tagged for Murder'
First Aired: 26 October 1967
Cast: Raymond Burr (Ironside), Don Galloway (Detective Sergeant Ed Brown), Don Mitchell (Marc Sanger), Barbara Anderson (Eve Whitfield), Gene Lyons (Commissioner Randall), Bruce Lee (Leon Soo)

Blondie

Episode: 'Pick on Someone Your Own Size'
First Aired: 1968
Regular Cast: Will Hutchins (Dagwood Bumstead), Patricia Harty (Blondie)
Guest Star: Bruce Lee

Here Come the Brides

Episode: 'Marriage, Chinese Style'
First Aired: 9 April 1969
Regular Cast: David Soul (Joshua Bolt), Bobby Sherman (Jeremy Bolt), Robert Brown (Jason Bolt)
Guest Star: Bruce Lee

Rejection

In 1968 Bruce was developing a script idea he had for a TV show called *The Warrior*. The basic concept was that a Shaolin monk wandered the plains of the Wild West and along the way he helped the needy and protected the weak using his Kung Fu skills. Bruce's idea was to show the true nature of Orientals through his martial arts and philosophical teachings. Through his celebrity connections his idea was passed on to Tom Kuhn who was in charge of television production at Warner Brothers. Kuhn suggested to Warner chief executives that they produce a pilot film for *The Warrior*, with Bruce in the lead role. They thought about it long and hard, but eventually came to the decision that Bruce Lee was too Oriental to play an Oriental in a lead role on prime-time television. Eventually the role was given to the extremely un-Oriental David Carradine and the show was renamed *Kung Fu*.

Bruce was absolutely devastated by the news that he had been rejected for the role and once more turned his attention to teaching martial arts to celebrities. He did, however, find happiness in 1969 with the birth of his daughter Shannon on 19 April.

Sterling Silliphant was a successful scriptwriter in Hollywood at the time and one way or another had come to hear about this little Chinese guy who could punch you from one inch and send you flying back six feet, and who could side-kick a 200lb man the full length of a swimming pool. Silliphant just had to meet this man. After contacting William Dozier, he eventually tracked Bruce down and began taking private lessons from him. Silliphant had written many successful scripts for Hollywood and wrote a part into *Marlowe* especially for Bruce. Silliphant continued to train with Bruce and whenever possible he would write his teacher into a film he was developing, either as an actor or as a fight coordinator.

Marlowe (1969)

Cast: James Garner (Phillip Marlowe), Gayle Hunnicut (Mavis Wald), Carrol O'Connor (Lieutenant Christy French), Rita Moreno (Dolores Gonzales), Jackie Coogan (Grant W Hicks), Bruce Lee (Winslow Wong)

Crew: Paul Bogart (Director), Sterling Silliphant (Writer)

Running Time: 96 mins

Story: Based on the novel *The Little Sister* by Raymond Chandler, James Garner plays private eye Phillip Marlowe, who is hired by a young girl to find her missing brother. Bruce Lee plays the oddly-named Winslow Wong, a henchman of the girl's gangster boyfriend. Midway through the movie Winslow turns up at Marlowe's office, offering him money to call off his investigation. When Marlowe refuses, Winslow destroys his entire office with his fists and feet. Shortly afterwards, on a rooftop of a restaurant, Marlowe taunts Winslow. When Winslow attempts a flying kick, Marlowe slyly side-steps and Winslow leaps off the edge of the roof.

Verdict: Bruce wasn't given much chance to show off his acting skills in the movie, but he did manage to demonstrate some great Kung Fu and the best office redesign you are ever likely to see. Bruce Lee 4/5 Film 3/5

The Wrecking Crew (1969)

Cast: Dean Martin (Matt Helm), Elke Sommer (Linka Karensky), Sharon Tate (Freya Carlson), Nancy Kwan (Yu Rang)

Crew: Phil Karlson (Director), Bruce Lee (Fight Choreography)

Walk in the Spring Rain (1970)

Cast: Ingrid Bergman (Libby Meredith), Anthony Quinn (Will Cade), Katherine Crawford (Ellen), Virginia Gregg (Ann Cade)

Crew: Guy Green (Director), Bruce Lee (Fight Choreographer)

Things Are Looking Up

Meanwhile, Bruce worked on his own script for *The Silent Flute* with Silliphant. They also worked on a pilot episode for a television show named *Longstreet*. The basic premise was that of an insurance investigator, Mike Longstreet, who was blinded in an explosion that also killed his wife. Longstreet then took the law into his own hands, tracking down the killer to a dockyard.

Just as he is about to be thrown off a pier by a gang of the killer's henchmen, Li Tsung steps in and rescues him, defeating the gang with his martial arts. Longstreet asks Li Tsung to teach him the 'way' so that he can defeat the murderer but is refused because he has the wrong motives for wanting to learn.

It took a while for the *Longstreet* series to get off the ground, so in the meantime Bruce decided to take a trip to Hong Kong with Brandon to arrange for his mother to live with him in America. Bruce couldn't believe his eyes when he stepped off the plane at Hong Kong's Kai Tak airport. Literally hundreds of fans had shown up to meet their idol. 'How could this be?' Bruce wondered. It turned out that *The Green Hornet* had been aired all across Asia and made Bruce a national hero. Not only that, but the show had been retitled *Kato*. TV stations, radio stations and newspapers were all over Bruce, asking for interviews and demonstrations of his Kung Fu. He appeared on one television show with young Brandon and although he disagreed with board-breaking he gave a demonstration of his power. Five boards were suspended on a rope for Bruce to break; he kicked the boards but only four broke, so he took the remaining one in his hand and broke it with a one-inch punch. Even Brandon got in on the act by demonstrating the moves his famous father had taught him.

Riding high on his new-found fame, Bruce asked his childhood friend Unicorn Chan to put out feelers for him with Shaw Brothers, the company for which Unicorn was working as a supporting actor. Unicorn told Bruce that Run Run Shaw was interested in Bruce doing a film for him, so Bruce quickly put a contract together which Unicorn Chan delivered personally. Bruce wanted HK$10,000 to appear in one film and also have the freedom to change any part of the script as he saw necessary and to choreograph all of the action. Run Run Shaw thought this was an absurd request and sent back his own counter-offer of a seven-year contract for HK$2,000 per film – it was the contract he offered to all his junior actors. Bruce declined his offer, returning to America where he was convinced his destiny lay despite his fame in the Far East.

On his return, *Longstreet* had been given the green light and filming commenced. This was the chance Bruce was waiting for. Now he would show the whole world the real meaning and philosophy behind his Jeet Kune Do and the Chinese 'way'.

In the short-lived *Longstreet*, Bruce appears in four episodes as Li Tsung, but what we see on screen is not a character created by Lee, it is the 'real' Bruce Lee. Bruce demonstrated his martial arts on more than one occasion and explained the philosophy behind his art. It is in this show that Bruce gave his speech about fluidity and that to be an effective fighter one must be like water.

Longstreet

Cast: James Franciscus (Mike Longstreet), Marilyn Mason (Nikki Bell), Peter Mark Richman (Duke

Paige), Ann Doran (Mrs Kingston), Bruce Lee (Li Tsung)
Crew: Charles S Dubin (Director), Bruce Lee (Fight Choreography)

Episode: 'The Way of the Intercepting Fist'
First Aired: 16 September 1971

Episode: 'Spell Legacy Like Death'
First Aired: 21 October 1971

Episode: 'Wednesday's Child'
First Aired: 11 November 1971

Episode: 'I See Said the Blind Man'
First Aired: 18 November 1971

A Brief History of the Chop Socky Movie

Before Bruce Lee completely changed the face of the Hong Kong film industry in 1971, the majority of films that were being made at the time were over-the-top, micro-budget Kung Fu movies with a lot of people flying around on wires. It is worth taking a look at the history of the Kung Fu movie to understand just how Bruce Lee revolutionised the genre.

It can be argued that Kung Fu movies are not really movies at all, but merely a showcase of stunts, brawls and acrobatics. Take the films of Jackie Chan for example: short on plot, big on action and mindless stunts, hardly contenders for an Oscar. However, what Chan's films lack in the acting department is more than made up for in every other aspect, from the beautiful locations to the balletic choreography, the quick-fire editing and the fantastic camera angles that make the action all the more believable. The films of Bruce Lee perhaps seem a little dated now when compared to the big budgets and high-calibre action of Chan's films, but what Bruce Lee did for Kung Fu films in the 1970s can be compared to what Jackie Chan has done for the action movies of the 1980s and 1990s.

Before Bruce Lee, the Chinese film industry was awash with badly shot, badly acted Kung Fu movies that were churned out *ad infinitum*, consisting of cheap films often based on Chinese folklore. The better films of the time were made by the Shaw Brothers' film company, headed by brothers Run Run and Run Me Shaw, but even their movies featured traditional Kung Fu, which more often than not depicted the hero as a superhuman, flying one-armed Kung Fu Master. Despite this, they still produced some classic Kung Fu movies, but they also made some that were dire. The Shaw Brothers' Movietown studios were located on the border of Kowloon and the New Territories, a giant of a studio with ten sound stages and 16 exterior sets. During its heyday, the Shaw studio could shoot up to seven films simultaneously. Their biggest star at the time was probably Jimmy Wang Yu, who starred in such movies as *The One Armed Boxer*, *Master of the Flying Guillotine* and *Zatoichi, The Blind Swordsman*. It has often been rumoured that Wang Yu was a high-ranking member of the Triads, the Chinese Mafia, and would years later use his Triad connections to persuade Jackie Chan to appear as the villain opposite his hero in *Killer Meteors* (1976) to help revive his dying career. He would again call on Chan to appear in the awful *Fantasy Mission Force* (1984) and finally, when his career had almost certainly died out, he asked Chan to appear in *Island of Fire* (1992), only this time also acquiring the talents of three other high-profile Hong Kong movie stars: Andy Lau, Samo Hung and Tony Leung.

The Shaw Brothers' studio was established in the

1920s, when Run Run and Run Me's father foreclosed a mortgage on a theatre. His brother Runji saw the foreclosure of the theatre as an ideal opportunity to stage a play he had written. Though the play was not as big a sell-out as Runji had anticipated, his enthusiasm led him to produce a film version that would have much more success. In 1924, the brothers moved to Singapore and set up a company that distributed the silent movies of Charlie Chaplin, Douglas Fairbanks and other American stars. The Shaw Brothers profited greatly from their newly found distribution network and soon began to expand, eventually opening a chain of around 100 cinemas and amusement parks. Then, to general disbelief, the Shaw Brothers did the unthink-able: they began to equip their new theatres with sound. Unfortunately, it was the time of the Second World War and the Japanese had other ideas for the Shaw empire, confiscating all of their theatres and parks. Not put off by their misfortune, the Shaw Brothers once more packed up shop and this time headed for Hong Kong, a bustling city that was an ideal setting for their film company. The company acquired the rights to some American pictures and the Shaw Brothers were back in business. As in Shanghai, the brothers began remaking historical period pieces.

By 1959, the Shaw Brothers were truly established in Hong Kong and come 1962 they were producing their first colour feature films. A lot of the films the brothers made were musicals, with hits such as *The Kingdom and the Beauty* and *Eternal Love*. The latter broke all box-office records for a Chinese-produced film. The Shaw

Brothers' theory on filmmaking at the time was to produce movies of all genres (love stories, musicals, period dramas and so on), then when a certain type of movie had a good box-office draw, they would churn out as many films as possible of that particular genre, very rarely spending over HK$300,000 per film. In 1964, the brothers made their first sword-fight movie and in 1968 they released the first real Kung Fu film in the shape of *The One Armed Swordsman*.

At the time of the release of *The One Armed Swordsman*, two of the top executives at the Shaw company were Ricky Uy, who would later leave to form Panasia Films, and Raymond Chow, who formed Golden Harvest.

Raymond Chow was born and raised in Hong Kong. In 1939 Raymond's father moved the family to Shanghai because he wanted young Raymond to have a Chinese education. In 1940 the Chow family were stranded in Shanghai when the Japanese started their attack on Pearl Harbor. Raymond finished his studies in 1958, graduating in journalism. During his last term at university he worked part-time for the United Press. Shortly afterwards, Raymond's father died, so the family moved back to Hong Kong. Raymond had gained a scholarship to the University of Missouri but he was now the family's only source of income, having to look after his mother and two younger brothers. After working at a few part-time jobs, Raymond finally landed a position with the Voice of America, setting up the company's radio and motion picture production section, which catered for overseas Chinese communities. Later that year, one of Raymond's university professors introduced him to Run Run Shaw. Shaw was looking for an advertising and publishing manager for his company and Raymond fitted the bill. Two months after joining the Shaw Brothers, Raymond viewed one of the company's productions and was horrified, so much so that he told Run Run he wanted to quit the job because he was sure that he couldn't sell the film. With that, Run Run Shaw decided that as well as being the advertising and marketing man, Raymond would also become a producer. His first production role at Shaw Brothers' was *Magnificent Concubine*, starring Li Li Hua, a remake of a traditional Chinese opera. The film did big business and won a prize at the Cannes Film Festival for production.

Raymond took on production of a number of movies and helped to set up the Clearwater Bay Studios. His input helped the Shaw Brothers to become the largest entertainment empire in Asia. After working for Run Run for eleven years, Raymond felt that it was time to move on and set up an independent film company of his own, so that he could produce the films that he wanted to see. In May 1970, Golden Harvest was born and would soon put the Shaw Brothers out of business.

One of Raymond Chow's first discoveries was Angela Mao Ying, a 19-year-old Chinese opera star, who would go on to appear as Bruce Lee's sister in *Enter the Dragon*. Not long after Raymond signed her, Bruce Lee appeared on Hong Kong television for a promotional tour for *The Green Hornet* television series.

SIMON KENNY

Raymond watched Bruce demonstrate his martial arts and decided that he wanted him to appear in his next production, *The Big Boss*.

The Big Time

Whilst Bruce was in America filming *Longstreet*, radio stations in Hong Kong were still calling him for interviews over the telephone. It is not certain whether Raymond Chow heard one of these conversations with Bruce or whether he had seen him appear on Hong Kong television, but either way he knew all about Bruce and wanted him to appear in one of his movies. He dispatched Liu Liang Hua, the wife of director Lo Wei, to the United States with a contract of employment for Bruce to sign and apparently told her not to come back unless she had his signature. Fortunately for Liu Liang Hua, Bruce signed the contract to appear in two movies produced by Golden Harvest for the sum of $15,000. The first of these two pictures was *The Big Boss*, which would be filmed in Pak Chong, Thailand. Raymond included a flight ticket in with the contract, not so much as a bonus for Bruce but as a safeguard that Bruce wouldn't fly to Hong Kong first and be tempted away by the Shaw Brothers, who were already making counter-offers.

The Big Boss (1971)

Cast: Bruce Lee (Cheng Chau-an), James Tien (Hsu Chien), Maria Yi (Chow Mei), Han Ying Chieh (the Big Boss), Tony Liu (Boss's Son), Li Quin (Lee Quin), Nora Miao (Miao)

Crew: Lo Wei (Director), Raymond Chow (Producer), Han Ying Chieh (Action Director), Joseph Koo (Music)

Notable Stuntmen/Extras: Lam Ching Ying

Running Time: 101 mins

Story: Cheng Chau-an arrives in Thailand with his Uncle Lu to work alongside his cousins at the local ice factory. Things are not what they seem, however, and it turns out that the ice factory is a cover-up for a drug-smuggling ring. On his first day at work Cheng accidentally breaks a block of ice that has a packet of dope inside. This is witnessed by two of Cheng's cousins. When the shift finishes, the two cousins are summoned to the manager's office where they are offered money to keep quiet about what they have seen. They refuse the money and are subsequently butchered by the manager's men and packed in ice. When they don't return home that evening, cousin Hsu Chien asks the manager about their whereabouts. Unhappy with the manager's explanation he and another cousin go to the house of Mi, the Big Boss of the title, to find out what is going on. The Boss is not happy with Hsu snooping around and as they are leaving he sends his son after them with a gang of heavily-armed henchmen. A badly choreographed fight scene follows (clearly choreographed by Han Ying Chieh and not Bruce Lee), in which Hsu and his cousin are killed, destined to wind up in the ice alongside the other two cousins.

The rest of the family get very concerned at this point and protest to the manager of the ice factory. A battle erupts between the workers and the manager's cohorts, but Cheng is reluctant to get involved – he has made a promise to his mother that he won't fight and he has sworn on a jade amulet that he wears around his neck. When the necklace is broken during the fight, Cheng unleashes his fists and feet of fury, taking out all of the bad guys single-handedly. The fight choreography here is far superior to the previous fight choreographed by Han Ying Chieh.

After the fight, the manager makes Cheng the new foreman of the factory. Cheng's cousins are overjoyed as they now think that something will be done to find out the mystery of their lost brothers. The manager, however, has other plans for Cheng and later that evening he invites him for dinner with the rest of his gang, hoping to get him on board with the illegal activities. Cheng gets drunk and forgets to ask the manager about his lost cousins; he awakes the next morning to find himself in a brothel. On returning to work, his cousins' make their feelings clear when he tells them that he forgot to ask about Hsu and the rest of the family. To try to regain the trust and respect of his cousins he goes back to the factory later that night to snoop around and investigate the disappearances himself. He is shocked to discover dope in the ice, but is even more horrified when he discovers the mutilated bodies of Hsu and the rest of the missing cousins. As he is leaving he comes face to face with a gang of thugs led by the Boss's son. This sets the scene for one of the most brutal and bloodthirsty fight scenes that Bruce Lee ever shot, culminating in the death of the Boss's son.

On returning to the house he shares with his cousins, Cheng discovers that the Boss's men have kidnapped the only female of the family, Chow Mei, and the rest of the family has been slaughtered in their sleep. Throwing his belongings into the river, Cheng makes up his mind that he must seek revenge for his murdered family and will sacrifice his own life in the name of justice. He arrives at the Boss's mansion eating a bag of prawn crackers, perhaps the final meal for a man facing death. With fist, feet and knives he mercilessly kills all of the Boss's guards. For the final show-down he faces the Boss, a man twice his age, in what must be the most mismatched fight in Bruce's film career. The fight, however, is remarkably good – probably due to Bruce Lee's intricate choreographing. He once said that he could make anyone look good on film and he demonstrates that here. Han Ying Chieh was a talented martial artist in his own right, but obviously at his age he was no match for Bruce Lee. Cheng finally defeats the Boss after a bloody and painful duel, collapsing in a heap on top of him. Chow Mei is released by one of the Boss's concubines and runs to the side of the wounded Cheng just as the police arrive. In Asia at the time of *The Big Boss* it was illegal for anyone committing crimes on screen to be seen to get away with it, even if their actions were justified, so we see Cheng arrested.

Background: Principal filming of *The Big Boss* began on 23 July 1970 in Pak Chong, Thailand. However, director Lo Wei did not arrive on set until five days after the shooting had commenced, replacing the film's initial director. This was to be the start of a heated and often violent three months between the stubborn Wei and the film's fiery-tempered star. Lo Wei was renowned for making low-budget movies and quickly filming the action scenes, but Bruce Lee was not going to let anyone get in the way of his quest for stardom, so the two often clashed. Although the action and fight choreography is credited to Han Ying Chieh, it is obvious that he only choreographed the fights that did not directly involve Bruce. A comparison between the fight with James Tien and the Boss's gang in the garden and any of Bruce Lee's fights clearly illustrates the difference in the choreographies.

Trivia: At the start of filming Bruce received a nasty cut to his finger whilst washing a glass. The bandage was visible on the first rushes of the film, so Bruce wore it throughout filming for continuity purposes.

Whilst on set, Bruce was challenged to a real-life brawl by a Thai Boxing champion. Not able to back down for fear of losing face, Bruce agreed to fight. After Bruce threw one devastating kick, the challenger submitted. Rumour has it that a cameraman shot the encounter, but Bruce made him destroy the film.

Yuen Wah performed most of the aerial acrobatic scenes in *The Big Boss*. Wah was a classmate of Jackie Chan at the Peking Opera School and has also appeared as the villain in some of Jackie's movies, most notably *Wheels on Meals*. Lam Ching Ying of *Mr Vampire* fame plays one of Bruce's cousins in the movie.

Lee Speaks: 'If I think that an action or a sentence is harmful to the film itself, even Raymond Chow will not be able to make me do it, unless he has enough reasons to convince me that he is right.'

Censorship: A publicity still for the film shows Bruce in the ice factory attacking a gang member who has a saw embedded in his forehead. It has often been debated whether or not the scene was actually shot. The scene doesn't exist in any of the released prints of the film but according to Bey Logan on the audio commentary for the UK DVD release, the scene was definitely shot. Sadly, as with a lot of the Hong Kong classics, the film was cut and the segment disposed of. After Bruce's character decides to avenge the deaths of his family, he once again returns to the brothel for a last moment of pleasure. The scene of Bruce pushing a prostitute onto the bed and then appearing naked behind a chair was considered too risqué for Hong Kong audiences at the time and was subsequently cut and has never been seen in later releases. Another cut scene was one of Bruce and James Tien's characters escaping from a burning cart in an alleyway after defeating the thugs from the gambling den.

Underlying Theme: According to Dan Inosanto, Bruce used *The Big Boss* to demonstrate his approach to mass fighting, that is, fighting against a gang. Obviously in real life to fight a gang of ten or more people just isn't realistic, but when facing maybe two or three opponents, it is possible for a skilful fighter to get out of the situation with his or her life. Paul Vunak, a Jeet Kune Do instructor under Dan Inosanto, demonstrates this art to great effect in his video *Mass Attack*. In *The Big Boss*, when faced with a gang of opponents, Bruce viciously attacks the first man. The object is to take out the strongest man first and visually intimidate the rest of the gang. Bruce also adopts the way of 'no-mindedness'. This is not 'not thinking', but more having complete awareness of his surroundings, not concentrating on his next move or technique, merely allowing 'it' to happen.

Verdict: This was the first of Bruce Lee's films for Golden Harvest, so he wasn't given the creative freedom that he wanted. Some of the action in the film is a little exaggerated, for example the scene where Cheng Chau-an punches a body through a wooden wall, leaving the outline of his body. Bruce said to Lo Wei, 'First you show me how to do it. If you can punch a person through a wall, I will follow your example. I don't think I can do it.' However, Bruce eventually agreed to shoot the scene to save wasted time on arguments, a decision he was later to regret. Bad decisions aside, the film has an interesting plot and some of Lee's most intense on-screen acting – the duel with the Boss's son and the final battle with the Big Boss himself being the most memorable. Film 3/5 Bruce Lee 3/5

The Big Boss opened in Hong Kong in October 1971 and broke all previous box-office records, far exceeding the expectations set by Raymond Chow and Golden Harvest. The audience went wild for Bruce. They were used to actors and stuntmen performing ridiculous feats of strength and agility, but here they had a hero who could really punch and really kick. Bruce had signed a contract with Raymond Chow to make two pictures so even before the first had premiered he had begun work on the second picture, *Fist of Fury*.

Fist of Fury (1972)

Cast: Bruce Lee (Chen Jeh), Nora Miao (Yuan), Jun Arimura (Suzuki's Bodyguard), Robert Baker (Petrov), Chen Fu Ching (Chao), Chin Sau (Tung), Han Ying Chieh (Feng Kwai Sher), Riki Hashimoto (Suzuki), Chung Hsin Huang (Tien), Lee Quin (Hsu), Lee Yin Chi (Li), Tony Liu (Chin), Lo Wei (Inspector), James Tien (Chang Chun Hsia), Ping-Ao Wei (Interpreter Wu)

Crew: Lo Wei (Director), Raymond Chow (Producer), Joseph Koo (Music), Bruce Lee (Action)

Notable Stuntmen/Extras: Jackie Chan, Yuen Wah, Lam Ching Ying

Running Time: 102 mins

Story: Chen Jeh arrives at the Ching Wu School of martial arts in Shanghai and is shocked to discover that his Master, Ho Yuan Chia, has passed away. He rushes to the cemetery for the funeral, where he sees his Master being buried; he cannot control his emotions and jumps into the grave, clawing at the coffin of his teacher. This is one of Bruce Lee's finest on-screen performances, demonstrating that he has the ability to act when necessary. The next day, the Ching Wu School holds a memorial for its late Master, but this is interrupted by a group of Japanese from the rival Honku School, led by the Chinese interpreter Wu. Wu gives the Ching Wu a plaque that reads 'Sick men of Asia' and challenges the Ching Wu to a fight, declaring that the Japanese are the stronger, more powerful race. Two of the fighters even go as far as to say that if any of the Chinese beat them they will eat the words on the plaque. Although Chen Jeh tries to rise to the challenge he is held back by one of his peers. The look in his eyes makes clear that he won't let them get away with insulting his Master's memory and the tension is such that you are literally willing Lee to fight.

The following day Chen Jeh arrives at the Honku School armed with the plaque and challenges them to a fight to prove who is the weakest race. He takes on the whole school with feet and fists. When the going gets too tough, he uses his weapon of choice, the nunchaku, with remarkable skill to attack the feet and ankles of his Japanese foes. After defeating the whole school, Chen

Jeh calls up the two fighters who said they would eat their words if they were beaten and literally forces the paper down their throats. As he leaves, Chen Jeh utters the immortal words, 'Now you remember this, we are not sick men.' When the film was first shown in Hong Kong the audience were literally jumping on their seats when Bruce defeated the Japanese and spoke this line. For years, they had been on the receiving end of oppression from the Japanese and now in Bruce Lee they had a national hero, who would stand up for his countrymen.

After the Master at the Japanese school, Suzuki, hears of Chen Jeh's visit he sends a gang out to the Ching Wu School to take revenge. However, Chen Jeh has gone for a stroll in the park. At the park Chen Jeh once more finds himself unleashing his 'fists of fury', this time because the park displays a sign outside that refuses entry to dogs and Chinese people – another political statement against racism that had audiences cheering.

On returning to the school, it is decided that Chen Jeh should leave for Shanghai the next morning. Later that night he overhears the cook discussing the Master's death with an accomplice. It becomes apparent that the two men are really Japanese and poisoned the teacher under the instructions of Suzuki. Chen Jeh kills the two schemers with his bare hands and leaves them hanging from a lamp post in the street outside. Chen swears vengeance for his murdered Master and, using a variety of disguises that demonstrate Bruce's character-acting ability, plots to seek revenge and kill Suzuki. Meanwhile, Suzuki has hired a Russian fighter to take care of Chen Jeh. As Suzuki's men leave to massacre the Chinese, Chen Jeh arrives at the Honku School to challenge Suzuki. After taking on and beating the remnants of Suzuki's students, Chen Jeh enters the garden area where he comes face to face with Petrov, the Russian strongman. In one of Bruce's best-choreographed fight scenes, he effortlessly beats Petrov with a combination of Kung Fu and Western Boxing. Now the path is clear for a final showdown with the leader.

Chen Jeh enters the Master's office and is nearly sliced in half by the katana-wielding Suzuki. Chen Jeh produces his nunchaku, quickly relieving Suzuki of his sword and, in a blistering hand-to-hand battle, sends him flying out into the garden with a flying kick to the throat. On returning to the Ching Wu School, Chen Jeh is arrested by the police and escorted out of the school, only to be faced with a firing squad. Chen Jeh defiantly stares down the firing squad then runs towards them and leaps into the air. The film is freeze-framed as we hear the fire of a dozen guns. As with *The Big Boss*, Chen Jeh could not be seen to get away with his crimes.

Background: Contrary to popular belief, *Fist of Fury* was shot almost entirely on a set constructed at Golden Harvest, the only exceptions being the outdoor location of Shanghai park and a small segment of the rickshaw scene, which were filmed in Macau. Bruce had a lot more control on this film than he did on *The Big Boss*, which made the production far superior to its predecessor. Tensions were still high between Bruce and director Lo Wei and once again filming was often interrupted due to disagreement. However, the film went on to out-gross *The Big Boss* and gave Bruce the opportunity and creative freedom to branch out and make his own films the way he wanted to.

Trivia: A young Jackie Chan appears in *Fist of Fury* as one of the Ching Wu School students. Jackie also performed the stunt when Bruce kicks Suzuki out into the garden in the final reel. At the time, it was Hong Kong cinema's highest wire fall. Ho Yuen Chia was a real person, but Chen Jeh was a fictitious character. A lot of the story, however, was based on real-life events surrounding Ho Yuen Chia's life.

Lee Speaks: 'I walk out and I say fuck you man, here I come. I leap up into the air and they stop the frame, bang, bang, bang, bang, bang, like Butch Cassidy and the Sundance Kid.'

Censorship: When first released in the UK, *Fist of Fury* passed the British Board of Film Censors virtually uncut, but later releases have shown a gradual increase in censorship. The most notable cuts have been of Bruce using his trademark weapon: the nunchaku.

Note: The film has now been released on DVD and all previous cuts have been restored.

Underlying Theme: Bruce Lee used this film to express his feelings against racial stereotyping. During his time in America, Bruce was often faced with racial barriers and fought all his life to bring them down. Warner Brothers rejected him for a television role because he looked too Oriental to play an Oriental. So with *Fist of Fury* he wanted the audience to understand that racism should not be tolerated. Bruce also wanted to bring to the audience's attention that being bound to a particular martial arts style or system can have negative effects on its practitioners. When the Japanese first threaten the Ching Wu School, they denounce the Chinese as the 'sick men of Asia', believing that the Japanese 'way' is the only one. Thus they are bound by tradition. Bruce demonstrates that it is not so much the style or system that makes the man succeed, but the individual himself or, more specifically, the individual's reasoning, integrity and/or beliefs.

Verdict: It is easy to see why *Fist of Fury* often tops the polls as Bruce's best film. The film has a great story, fantastic sets and the most realistic fight sequences you are ever likely to see. Bruce at his furious fighting best. Film 4/5 Bruce Lee 4/5

Fist of Fury was another smash hit, out-grossing all the previous records set by *The Big Boss*. Tickets were even being sold on the black market for up to 20 times their face value. Bruce Lee had truly arrived and, with his Golden Harvest contract completed, every producer in town wanted him to appear in their movies. Run Run Shaw was pulling his hair out – he had had the opportunity to sign Bruce way before Raymond Chow had got his hands on him but had failed to see Bruce's potential. Run Run was now desperate to get Bruce for one of his films. First he made Bruce an offer of approximately $200,000 and when that failed he sent Bruce a blank cheque. But Bruce Lee had his own ideas – he wanted to write, produce, direct and star in his next film. With *The Big Boss* and *Fist of Fury* there hadn't been a script, just a rough outline of a story with changes being made as filming went along. Now Bruce had the chance to make the films of his choice. So with Raymond Chow as his partner, Bruce formed his own film company, Concorde, and began work on his third motion picture, *Way of the Dragon*.

Way of the Dragon (1972)

Cast: Bruce Lee (Tang Lung), Nora Miao (Chen Ching Hua), Chuck Norris (Colt), Bob Wall (Fred), Whang In Sik (Japanese Fighter), Jon T Benn (Boss), Unicorn Chan (Jimmy), Tony Liu (Tony)

Crew: Bruce Lee (Director)

Notable Stuntmen/Extras: Jackie Chan, Yuen Wah, Lam Ching Ying

Running Time: 95 mins

Story: Tang Lung, a country bumpkin from Hong Kong, arrives in Rome to help out a friend who is being threatened by a local mob boss who wants to buy her restaurant business. After hearing Miss Chen Ching Hua's story, Tang Lung is taken to the restaurant where

Miss Chen's employees are in the alley being taught
Karate by Jimmy, one of the waiters, to defend them-
selves against the mob. Whilst Tang Lung is in the restroom the mob arrive at the restaurant led by the Boss's
right-hand man. Tang Lung comes out of the restroom
and bumps right into the somewhat camp mobster,
apologising as he does not know who he is. Miss Chen
is furious, regarding Tang Lung as useless. Her opinion
is soon to change. The next night, four of the gang
arrives at the restaurant and bully two of the waiters.
Jimmy challenges the gang to a fight, but is quickly
knocked unconscious. As another waiter steps forward,
he is held back by Tang Lung. In a dazzling display of
Chinese boxing, Tang Lung knocks all four gang
members unconscious much to the disbelief of Miss
Chen and the waiters.

Hearing of Tang Lung, the mob boss hires a hit man
to get rid of him. When that fails, the boss threatens to
send Tang Lung back to Hong Kong. The gang arrives
at the restaurant and Tang Lung is led out into the alley.
After quickly disarming the gunman, he takes on the
whole gang, using not one but two pairs of nunchaku.
He returns to the restaurant and angrily tells the boss to
leave the place alone. Reluctantly, the boss agrees and
makes his way out.

By now, the boss is seething with anger and wants to
seek revenge on Tang Lung. With the camp sidekick, he
devises a plan to trick Tang Lung into a meeting at the
famous Roman Coliseum, where he will have three of
the world's top martial artists waiting to kill him.
Arriving at the Coliseum with the waiters, Tang Lung

soon realises that it is a trap when he sees two of the fighters walking towards him. In the ensuing fight, Tang Lung quickly overpowers one and then the other. Leaving the waiters to finish them off, Tang Lung makes his way into the Coliseum for the final duel with Colt, played by world Karate champion Chuck Norris.

This is the greatest fight scene ever filmed. It clearly expresses Bruce's art of Jeet Kune Do – adapting to your opponent. Initially Tang Lung is overpowered by the much bigger Colt, but after changing his approach and giving a fantastic display of Jeet Kune Do's broken rhythm, Tang takes the upper hand. The epic battle ends with Tang Lung breaking the neck of the brave American. Out of respect, Tang Lung covers the lifeless body with his jacket and then goes to face the boss.

The boss has a gun, while Tang Lung only has wooden darts he has carved – it doesn't look good for Tang Lung, but fortunately the police arrive in the nick of time to arrest the boss. The final shot has Tang Lung walking down the road like the 'Man With No Name', as a cheesy voiceover from one of the waiters says, 'Wherever he may wander…'

Background: Before filming began, Bruce read as many books as possible on all aspects of filmmaking, from direction to producing to editing and lighting – he wanted this to be the best picture he could possibly make. He arrived in Rome on 4 May 1972 to begin location shooting, accompanied by Raymond Chow and cameraman Nashinoto Tadashi. Three days later the rest of the cast and crew arrived and for the next week they filmed all the outdoor location shots before returning to Hong Kong for the interiors. The plot of *Way of the Dragon* is very thin, but since it was only intended for the Asian market, Bruce emphasised the comedy and action rather than the story. The final battle with Chuck Norris took up more than forty pages!

Trivia: After the enormous success of both *The Big Boss* and *Fist of Fury*, Lee knew he had to do something extraordinary with *Way of the Dragon*, so he decided to shoot the film in Rome. It was the first Hong Kong production to be filmed overseas. The film was never intended for international release and was not released in America until after Bruce's death – where it was marketed as a sequel to *Enter the Dragon* and renamed *Return of the Dragon*.

The fight inside the Coliseum was filmed on a specially constructed set at Golden Harvest because filming inside the Coliseum was strictly forbidden. However, Bruce did manage to sneak a camera inside the Coliseum to film the exterior shots. World heavyweight Karate champion, Joe Lewis, was originally approached to play the part of Colt, but he refused on the grounds that he didn't think it would be believable that his character would be beaten by a little Chinese man. Many believe it was because he was too slow to fight opposite Bruce and didn't want to embarrass himself.

Lee Speaks: 'It is really a simple plot of a country

[boy] going to a place where he cannot speak the language but somehow comes out on top because he honestly and simply expressed himself.'

Censorship: *Way of the Dragon* is the most censored of all of Bruce Lee's films and the official UK release has been cut so much that the majority of the fight sequences just don't make sense. The first major cut occurs when Bruce takes on the gang in the back alley behind the restaurant. He knocks the first fighter out with a spinning kick to the head. He then knocks out another thug who thinks he can out-box Bruce. Then miraculously all of the gang end up on the floor unconscious with no explanation as to how they got there. Later in the film Bruce goes outside the restaurant for another confrontation with the gang. This time he uses an assortment of weapons, including two pairs of nunchaku simultaneously. Again, the British Board of Film Censors thought that this scene was too violent for the British viewer and cut it completely – an outrageous cut when you look at some of the more graphic scenes of violence prevalent in movies such as *American History X*. When Tang Lung heads for the Coliseum for the final showdown with Colt he is first confronted by Colt's student Fred and a Japanese fighter. Both of these fights have had segments trimmed, including a kick from Bruce to the testicles of Bob Wall. Painful? Yes. Worthy of censorship? No.

Finally, the duel with Chuck Norris sees the BBFC getting scissor-happy once more, completely taking the grit and the reality of battle out of the final reel. After getting his butt seriously kicked by Norris, Bruce changes his approach, demonstrating the true essence of Jeet Kune Do. After toying with Norris for a while, Bruce backs his opponent against the wall. A thoroughly exhausted and demoralised Norris attempts to fight back. In the original footage, Bruce breaks Norris's arm and leg, then grips his neck and breaks it. Obviously we wouldn't want every Tom, Dick and Harry going around breaking people's arms and legs, so the BBFC decided to cut the scene, leaving the audience wondering why Norris is limping and holding his arm. The film has been left intact by virtually every country in which it has been released, so why has it been cut so dramatically in Britain? Each release sees the censors cut more and more from Lee's films, so my advice would be to buy *Way of the Dragon* now before it is trimmed down to three minutes. Bizarrely, the American release has had the scenes of Bruce arriving at the airport cut but the fight scenes left intact!

Note: *Way of the Dragon* has now been released on DVD and contains all of the cut scenes.

Underlying Theme: With *Way of the Dragon*, Bruce truly expressed his philosophy of 'having no way, as way'. During his fight with Chuck Norris, he initially gets a serious beating because he is too rigid in his approach. Norris is also rigid, with the result that the two fighters land an equal number of blows on one another. However, Norris's size and power get the better of Bruce. Bruce therefore decides to change his approach and adopts the 'style of no style', constantly varying his attacks and using a broken rhythm, much to the distress of the tiring Norris.

Bruce also wanted to get across the point that all martial arts are effective no matter where they originate from. During his early years in America, Bruce would often find himself in trouble for criticising traditional arts such as Karate or Tae Kwon Do, but that wasn't because he thought they were worthless – he just believed that people should open their minds and seek to learn the other arts. In one scene outside the restaurant, all but one of the waiters is practising Karate. When Bruce asks the waiter why he isn't practising, he replies 'because it is foreign'. Bruce scolds the waiter, telling him that it doesn't matter where an art comes from, if it helps you in a fight then it is worth knowing.

Bruce also wanted to show that you should respect and honour your fellow man, no matter what your personal feelings toward him. A good example is when Tang Lung covers the body of Colt with his jacket after the final battle.

Verdict: Thin on plot and character development, *Way of the Dragon* may be dated by today's standards but the fight scenes are the most realistic you will see anywhere. Bruce really played this role for laughs. This is my personal favourite of all of Bruce Lee's films, but my rating reflects my unbiased opinion. Film 2/5 Bruce Lee 3/5

An Interview with Jon Benn

Jon Benn was a co-star in *Way of the Dragon*. I conducted this interview with him in June 1998 at his Bruce Lee Café in Hong Kong.

Simon: Jon, how did you first get involved in acting and how did you get involved in *Way of the Dragon*?

Jon: What happened is I met Raymond Chow at a cocktail party and he said, 'Would you like to be in a movie with Bruce Lee?' I didn't really know who Bruce Lee was at that time, but anyway I said, 'Sure, I've not done that before.' The next morning he picked me up at 8 o'clock and by 8:30 we had shot the first scene and that was my first experience of acting. Since then I have appeared in 32 movies – the last one was *Ghosts Can't Do It* – that was the most fun.

Simon: What was it like working with Bruce Lee?

Jon: He was a very fun guy. He was always joking and having a ball, and every day was a party on the set. He loved to show off. He knew he was the best and he was constantly showing off. I'd be standing there smoking a cigar and he would come up next to me and 'boom' he would kick the ash off my cigar! He was so accurate, right up to your face and you would feel the air but he wouldn't touch you. Very accurate. He could do it five hundred times in a row and then jump up and kick a light bulb out. He was always stretching and then falling down and landing on two fingers, do a hundred push-ups. But he did that to show off. He was very direct though and knew what he wanted and he got what he wanted. He was a very good director.

Simon: It was quite a feat in those days to do all that Bruce Lee did on *Way of the Dragon*.

Jon: Yes, he wrote it, produced it, directed it and starred in it. He was a really great guy, someone to look up to.

Simon: Were there any scuffles or challenges on the set?

Jon: No, it was very straightforward. There was one time when they had a big fight in my office in the film and they had picked up some guys from Chungking Mansions; backpackers. Just to be extras. About ten of them. One guy was a big American and he was supposed to hit this little Chinese guy on the head and the guy forgot to move his head.

He was supposed to get married at 3 o'clock that afternoon and the whole cast including Bruce went to the wedding but that guy went there with a fat lip. [Laughs] But nothing involving Bruce. He would demonstrate the one-inch punch on a guy as big as me and the guy would fly into a bunch of mattresses. One time I saw him hit this 300lb punching bag about five feet high. I mean, people couldn't even move it. They would hit it and it would move a little bit or kick it and it would move a little bit and Bruce said 'watch this,' and he goes 'bam!' – the son of a bitch flew all the way to the ceiling. Hit the ceiling! I couldn't believe it. He was the most powerful guy I ever met. Incredible. He just knew where the energy would come from. His Jeet Kune Do was a combination of a lot of things and it worked. Well, it sure worked for him anyway.

Simon: Bruce wasn't a very big man; did he look tiny to you?

Jon: Well, he was 5ft 7in but he only weighed 138 pounds, which was all muscle. He was a little guy but you appreciated that when he flexed, he wasn't so little.

Simon: It sounds like you really enjoyed yourself?

Jon: Yeah, I enjoyed working with him and it was good to get to know him. I got to be pretty good friends with him. I used to have a little beach house in Lan Tau years ago, and invited him and Linda and the two kids over there to get away from the autograph hunters. Back then, it had clean water and a nice beach. He loved it.

Simon: Do you still get recognised from your role in *Way of the Dragon*?

Jon: Yes, still after 25 years. Not a day goes by when some Chinese guy on the MTR or a cab driver will say 'Lee Siu Lung, Kung Fu,' which means 'Bruce Lee, Kung Fu' because my name is Kung Fu. That is the name they gave me because in the movie one of the guys says to me, 'I know a guy who does Kung Fu' and I say 'Kung Fu?' They also use that line in a television commercial so everybody still calls me Kung Fu. [Laughing]

One time a few years ago I was in New York, walking down 42nd Street. I was with a couple of guys and I noticed they were playing a movie across the street and there was a big long queue of black guys stood outside. Walking by, one of them said, 'Hey man, there's "the Big Boss"!' [Laughing] They were asking me all sorts of questions and then asked me to go in with them and see the movie, be their guest. I said thanks but I have already seen the movie about fifty times. Anyway I thanked them and turned to walk away and I get a tap on the shoulder and I'm looking at the belt buckle of the biggest black cop I ever saw. He had to be 7ft 5in tall and he says, 'I hear you were in that movie with Bruce Lee?' and I say 'Yes, Sir.' And he said, 'Come in here – I want you to meet some friends.' He took us in a bar. In New York the bars close at 2 o'clock in the morning, but we were in there till 5 o'clock in the morning, the three of us.

Another time we were in Paris and I noticed that the movie was playing at some theatre, so I said we should go down and take a look. We went in and found out that the movie had been playing at that theatre for eight years straight!

Simon: There is a scene in the movie when Bruce shoves you into your chair with his shoulder. That looked quite powerful. Did it hurt?

Jon: It did really hurt. But I got to tell you that me and the chair flipped over backwards, so for take two we had these two big guys behind the chair holding it! [Laughs] It did kinda knock the wind out of me.

Simon: Did you get along well with Chuck Norris and Bob Wall?

Jon: Yes. Actually I bumped into Chuck a few years ago in Manila. He was doing a film out there. We went out and had dinner afterwards and I said to him, 'Tell me, if you and Bruce were really going to fight to the death, who would win?' and he said, 'No doubt about it, Bruce would.' This is coming from a guy who retired eight times world champion, undefeated. Everybody had a lot of respect for Bruce, and Chuck was good. No doubt about it.

Simon: What do you think of the movie now?

Jon: I still like it. We show it here all the time. We show all his movies here and documentaries.

Simon: Finally, is there still a big interest in Bruce Lee in Hong Kong? All of the people I have met so far don't care that much.

Jon: All the people I have met care a lot. It seems to me that there is a lot of interest. A lot of people come in here now. People come all the way from Taiwan and all over.

As *Fist of Fury* had smashed all records set by *The Big Boss*, so *Way of the Dragon* out-grossed all records set by *Fist of Fury*. Now the money really started rolling in and Bruce could afford all the luxuries that he and Linda desired. He purchased a two-storey house in Cumberland Road, Kowloon, and, although it wasn't much compared to Hollywood standards, by Hong Kong standards it was a mansion. He purchased Italian designer suits and a top of the range hi-fi system.

Despite his success, Bruce was beginning to feel quite pressured. His weight was plummeting and he was eating less and less. He could no longer go out in public without being mobbed by fans, or challenged to a fight by somebody wishing to make a name for himself by beating the 'King of Kung Fu'. Bruce had worked hard to become successful and a bigger star than James Coburn and Steve McQueen, but now the pressure of stardom was telling on him. Rather than relax and take time off to adjust to his new-found status, Bruce plunged himself straight back into work and began filming *Game of Death*. This was to be Bruce's crowning glory, a film that would finally reveal the real truth of Jeet Kune Do and give an insight into his philosophy. Bruce began filming the final fight scenes for *Game of Death* first, because, although he had a rough outline of the script, it was by no means complete, so he would get what footage he could canned whilst he worked on the rest of the script. Whilst shooting *Game of Death*, Bruce was besieged with offers from all over the world to star in movie after movie. He had offers from Thailand, Taiwan, Singapore and Japan. He was offered two million dollars to star in two pictures made by an Hungarian film company, and there was an offer from Carlo Ponti for an unspecified sum to star in a film with his wife Sophia Loren. However, shooting on *Game of Death* was halted when Bruce was made an offer by Warner Brothers to star in an American-made feature that would give Bruce complete control over all of the action. This was the offer Bruce had been waiting for, to star in a US film and get the chance to show his art to the world.

Enter the Dragon (1973)

Cast: Bruce Lee (Lee), John Saxon (Roper), Jim Kelly (Williams), Ahna Capri (Tania), Shieh Kien (Han), Bob Wall (O'Hara), Angela Mao Ying (Su Lin), Betty Chung (Mei Ling), Geoffrey Weeks (Braithwaite), Peter Archer (Parsons), Bolo (Yang Tze)

Crew: Robert Clouse (Director), Raymond Chow, Paul Heller, Fred Weintraub (Producers), Lalo Schiffrin (Music)

Notable Stuntmen/Extras: Jackie Chan, Samo Hung, Yuen Biao, Yuen Wah, Lam Ching Ying

Running Time: 98 mins

Story: An intelligence officer named Braithwaite arrives at a Shaolin temple and asks Shaolin monk, Lee, to go undercover at a martial arts tournament on a remote island to investigate Han, a renegade from Lee's Shaolin temple. Initially Lee refuses, but when he learns from Braithwaite that his sister had committed suicide rather than face being raped by Han's henchmen, he agrees. It becomes apparent that Han's tournament is a cover-up to recruit new talent into his organisation of drug peddling and illegal prostitution. Also attending the tournament are Roper, a compulsive gambler who is in trouble with the mob, and Williams, an old army buddy of Roper's who constantly finds himself on the wrong side of the law. Arriving at the island, Lee soon hooks up with Mei Ling, another intelligence operative placed on the island by Braithwaite. Mei Ling tells Lee of Han's activities and where things happen on the island. Later, Lee dresses in a black catsuit and goes out into the night to investigate. He doesn't get far before he is spotted by some guards. Lee effortlessly kills the guards and makes his way back inside Han's palace. In the meantime, Roper goes out onto his balcony to get some fresh air; he notices the silhouetted figure of Lee climbing a wall, just as one of Han's guards notices Williams, who is also outside. Han's rules strictly forbid anybody to be out at night.

The next day at the tournament Han has his body-guard Bolo teach his guards a lesson for letting someone wander around outside. Bolo takes delight in mercilessly killing four guards whilst the shocked spectators look on. Han suspects that Williams is the spy and asks him if he is shocked. 'Only at how sloppy your men were,' Williams replies.

The tournament begins and both Williams and Roper quickly defeat their opponents. Next is Lee whose opponent is Han's henchman O'Hara, the person responsible for his sister's death. A flashback shows how and why his sister died as Lee strikes out at O'Hara with lightning speed. The fight is very one-sided and Lee easily defeats O'Hara, knocking him to the ground. Lee jumps into the air and comes down with a foot stomp that breaks O'Hara's neck.

After the day's proceedings, Williams is summoned to Han's office where he is accused of being a spy. Williams tells Han that he doesn't take kindly to the accusation and a fight erupts. Han kills Williams with an iron hand that until now has been covered with a glove. Later that night Lee goes out once more, this time finding an underground cavern where he witnesses cells full of prisoners – girls being kept as prostitutes – and drugs being manufactured. He locates a radio room and puts in a call to base to request back-up, but the radio sets off an alarm. He is soon swarmed by Han's guards and must fight for his life using all of the skills he has learnt at the Shaolin temple. After defeating 30 or so guards with the use of his hands, feet and some weapons acquired from the guards, Lee makes a dash to escape but finds himself trapped in a cave with steel doors. Han looks down into the cave and congratulates Lee on his performance as he sits cross-legged awaiting his punishment. Later that evening Han shows Roper around his grounds and tells him of his operation, hoping that Roper will join the syndicate. Roper, always one for a deal, seems keen on the idea until he sees the lifeless body of Williams hanging over a vat of acid. Roper declines Han's offer and, like Lee, is locked up to face the consequences.

The next morning Roper and Lee are led out to the tournament ground to meet their fate. Neither of them is aware of what the other has done. Han wants the two to fight to the death. Lee seems willing but Roper wisely rejects the suggestion, so Han calls on Bolo to take care of them. Lee steps forward to take up the challenge, but instead Roper takes him on, eventually killing the giant with a kick to the heart. Han orders some of his guards to kill Roper and Lee, but they are no match and are soon put out of action, so Han orders more and more men to attempt to kill the pair. Meanwhile, Mei Ling has set free the prisoners from the underground cavern. They run out into the grounds and a massive battle ensues between them and Han's men.

Lee moves in to kill Han, who makes a run for it. At his museum, Han changes his iron hand for a hand of razor-sharp knives. Lee takes quite a few cuts from the knives, before Han hides in a maze of mirrors. The mirrors make it impossible for Lee to distinguish between the real Han and his reflection, so Lee starts to break the mirrors with his fists. Eventually, Lee spots the real Han and with a magnificent side kick sends him flying back onto his own spear.

A tired Lee goes outside where he catches sight of an exhausted Roper. He gives him the thumbs up as military back-up arrives by helicopter.

Background: Filming commenced in January 1973 on what would be the film that made Bruce Lee a worldwide superstar. For the next four months Bruce put everything he had into making the film the best that it could possibly be and it paid off. Even now, almost 35 years after it was made, *Enter the Dragon* remains the most famous martial arts film ever and is the film for which Bruce Lee is most remembered.

Trivia: Whilst filming his fight scene against Bob Wall (O'Hara), Bruce Lee received a serious cut to his hand. The action called for Bruce to kick two bottles from Wall's hands but Wall held onto them longer than necessary, resulting in the serious injury. Extras on the set immediately began speculating and spreading rumours that Wall had injured Bruce deliberately, and before long Bruce got to hear about them. Allegedly Bruce told a number of people that he was going to 'kill' Bob Wall, otherwise he would 'lose face'. ('Face' is a Chinese term for respect.) The rest of the shoot was very tense but, fortunately for Wall, went without incident. According to Wall, however, Bruce never threatened to kill him and it was merely a rumour.

Bruce was challenged many times on the set of *Enter the Dragon* by extras and stuntmen hoping to boost their ego and status. He generally laughed off these challenges, although on more than one occasion had to accept the challenges otherwise he would 'lose face'. The encounters generally didn't last very long; usually Bruce would only hit his opponent once and not at full power, just to warn them and show them that he meant business.

Jackie Chan has the pleasure of having his neck broken by Bruce Lee during the underground cavern sequence. Yuen Wah doubled for Bruce Lee during the acrobatic scenes in the movie. The film was made for a mere $850,000 dollars and has grossed to date over $200 million. In comparison, *The Godfather*, which was released in the same year, was made for $17 million and has grossed approximately $88 million. The film is still in Warner Brothers' top ten highest-grossing movies of all time.

Lee Speaks: '*Enter the Dragon* should make it. This is the movie that I am proud of because it is made for the US audience as well as the Oriental. This is definitely the biggest movie I've ever made. I'm excited to see what will happen. I think it's going to gross $20 million in the US.'

Censorship: A small segment at the beginning of the film sees Lee talking to the head monk of the Shaolin temple. This scene was written by Bruce and is a great insight into the philosophy by which he led his life. The scene also goes a long way to explaining the reason behind Lee smashing all the mirrors during the final battle with Han. The scene has been restored for the special-edition release, with Bruce Lee historian John Little dubbing Bruce's voice because the original soundtrack was damaged.

In the original release of the film Bruce Lee used a pair of nunchaku to defeat some of Han's guards during the underground cavern scene. The scene was also included in the television premiere in the early eighties but has since been removed from all UK prints. If you look closely at this scene you can see that Bruce barely blinks his eyes, this is because the film speed had to be slowed down to catch the nunchaku. Bruce's proficiency with the weapon had increased that much since shooting *Fist of Fury* that he was just too fast for the camera.

Note: *Enter the Dragon* has now been released on DVD and contains all of the cut scenes.

Underlying Theme: Probably Bruce Lee's most philosophical film, *Enter the Dragon* has many memorable lessons. The most important is the 'art of fighting without fighting' lesson he gives to Parsons on the junk. As with most martial artists who are confident in their abilities, Bruce believed that the best way to deal with an aggressor is just to walk away. If that isn't possible, one alternative is to trick him into believing he has the upper hand, while knowing in your own mind that you have simply let him off the hook. Another alternative is to use 'the art of fighting without fighting', thus getting the aggressor out of threat range without using force. Another lesson in the film comes from the oft-quoted line Bruce speaks to his young student at the Shaolin temple, 'Don't think, feel. It is like a finger pointing a way to the moon.' When the student stares at Bruce's finger he gets a slap on the head and Bruce continues, 'Don't concentrate on the finger or you will miss all the heavenly glory.' What Bruce was saying is that you must open your mind to all that is around you; to merely concentrate on the finger is to miss the full picture. Bruce believed that to express yourself honestly is the most difficult thing for a human being to do and with *Enter the Dragon* he wanted to get this message across.

Verdict: A martial arts epic of magnificent proportions, *Enter the Dragon* is still the yardstick by which all martial arts films are measured. Considered the 'James Bond' of martial arts movies, *Enter the Dragon* has it all: a good cast, a good plot, a funky 1970s soundtrack and classic martial arts choreography. It is just a shame that we didn't get to see Bruce and Bolo square off. Film 5/5 Bruce Lee 5/5

Filming on *Enter the Dragon* was completed in April 1973 and released worldwide on 26 July to critical acclaim, subsequently making Bruce Lee the most famous actor on the planet. Film producers were clamouring to sign him for their next feature film, but, unbeknown to them, he had died six days before the film's release.

In January 1969 Bruce wrote his chief personal aim in a letter to himself: 'I Bruce Lee will be the first highest-paid Oriental superstar in the United States. In return I will give the most exciting performances and render the best of quality in the capacity of an actor. Starting in 1970 I will achieve worldwide fame and from then onward till the end of 1980 I will have in my possession $10,000,000. I will live the way I please and achieve inner harmony and happiness.'

With the release of *Enter the Dragon*, Bruce Lee was truly on his way to achieving his goal. Unfortunately, it was never to be.

The Death of Bruce Lee

When Bruce Lee died on 20 July 1973, the world was stunned. How could someone so fit die at the age of 32? Since his death there have been many rumours as to the cause, but the official version recorded on his death certificate was 'Death by Misadventure' due to a cerebral oedema caused by sensitivity to a painkiller. But was this the real cause of his death? Here are some of the more popular theories.

Was Bruce Lee Murdered by the Triads?

Many people believe that Bruce was killed by the Triads (the Chinese Mafia), because he wouldn't make films for them or refused to pay them protection money. The Triads have been a prevalent threat to the Hong Kong cinema industry for years and have threatened the livelihoods of some of the biggest stars. Bruce Lee had dealt with their kind before, when he was a teenager. He had stood up to them then and he would stand up to them again. He wasn't going to let anyone take something from him that he had worked so hard for, no matter who they were. Could it be possible that the Triads had Bruce killed because he refused to pay them protection money or make films for them? It is possible, but doubtful. Bruce was just too big a star. It would be like the Triads murdering Jackie Chan today – he is simply too well known, which is why Jackie can go on anti-Triad marches in Hong Kong and refuse to pay them anything. Instead, the Triads stick to actors who are not as well known so that they do not bring attention to their organisation.

Was Bruce Lee Killed by a Mystery Kung Fu Master?

It is well known that Bruce had upset a number of martial artists. He had angered the Chinese fraternity with his teaching of Kung Fu to Westerners and he had offended other groups by degrading their martial art. Could one of these Masters have killed him, perhaps by using a delayed death strike?

Dim Mak is an ancient martial art that is concerned with strikes to the vital points or pressure points on the human body. It was created by the same man who devised the original Tai Chi form many centuries ago and the results of striking at the vital points can be knockout, death, or delayed death. According to the theories of acupuncture, the body has a circulating life force (Chi) that travels around the body through invisible channels called meridians. Along these meridians are certain points that needles can be inserted into, to alter the flow of Chi to cure illnesses and disease. However, these points can also be used to cause adverse effects, such as a disruption in the life force. I can bear witness to the fact that these points can cause a knockout because I have been on the receiving end of a demonstration and was instantly knocked unconscious. However, I can neither prove nor disprove the theory that these attacks can kill, because I didn't want to go that far in the demonstration. Nonetheless, I have no doubt that these attacks can kill. Many of these vital points can be neurologically linked to the vital organs and when attacked can result in disruption to the particular organ. It is believed that the pressure involved during the attack can determine the length of time it will take for the organ to fail. It has been suggested that some ancient Master in the art of Dim Mak hit Bruce with a delayed death touch that caused him to have a cerebral oedema months later. It is not impossible that this could have happened, but in my opinion it is doubtful because in his later years it was very difficult for anyone to get close to him. He had become a huge celebrity and had bodyguards with him wherever he went.

Was Bruce Lee Poisoned?

This is another popular theory and one that could hold some truth. I do not want to go into details, because to name anyone would have legal implications. Let us just say that there were undoubtedly certain people who would perhaps have benefited from the death of Bruce Lee and others who had something to hide from him. Before Bruce Lee's fatal collapse in July 1973, he had earlier passed out in May whilst dubbing the soundtrack for *Enter the Dragon*. On first inspection it appeared that Lee had had an epileptic fit, but his brain had swelled drastically just like it would again on the day he died. The effects were the same as if he had been poisoned. Bruce was known to eat hashish cookies to relax – it would not have been difficult for somebody to taint his supply with poison of some sort.

Did Bruce Lee Become a Recluse?

It was circulated shortly after Bruce's death that he was tired of the pressures of fame, or that he had received death threats and decided to retreat to a Shaolin temple to seek spiritual enlightenment. He would reappear again ten years to the day to share his enlightenment with his followers. Well, he is 25 years late if this is the case and by all accounts Bruce Lee was a very punctual person, so I think we can dispel this theory. Many people do not want to believe that their hero is gone and this rumour is common among the cult of dead celebrities – Jim Morrison and Elvis Presley, for example.

Did Bruce Lee Commit Suicide?

No. It has been suggested that Bruce Lee knew he would never see old age and that his days on Earth were numbered so he took his own life. Bruce Lee was a very hard-working, meticulous human being. He had an enormous amount of vitality and plans for his future. He was at the pinnacle of his career, a career that he had worked so hard for during his life. He was potentially the highest-paid actor in the world and was finally able to make films on his own terms. *Game of Death* was to be his crowning glory, a multi-level film that would introduce Bruce's philosophy to the world and show the true meaning of Jeet Kune Do. I think if Bruce were to commit suicide he would have at least finished his dream project. Bruce Lee seemed to know that he wouldn't be around too much longer – he reportedly said to Robert Clouse's wife on the set of *Enter the Dragon* that he wouldn't live to see his next birthday. But did he kill himself? No, definitely not!

Was Bruce Lee Cursed?

The Chinese are a very superstitious people and many of them believe that bad omens were responsible for the death of Bruce Lee. When Bruce was born in 1940 his mother had one of his ears pierced and gave him the female name Sai Fon, which means 'Little Phoenix'. This was to protect her child from evil spirits who are believed to take the souls of young children, especially the males. For the first few years of his life, Bruce was referred to as Sai Fon and was dressed in girl's clothing so that the spirits would not take him. However, a lot of Chinese people believe that you cannot outsmart the spirits and if they want to take someone, they will eventually. When Bruce moved into his house on Cumberland Road, it was in an area of Hong Kong called Kowloon Tong, which translates literally as 'Nine Dragon Pond'. The two previous owners of Bruce's house had both met with unfortunate circumstances and it was believed by many that the house carried bad luck. A Feng Shui expert had told Bruce that the house was bad luck and not facing the correct way for true harmony and advised him to place a mirror on the roof of the house to ward away evil and bad luck. Two days before he died the mirror was blown off the roof during a storm. Was this just a coincidence or could it have been a curse from the 'Nine Dragons', because they didn't want 'the Little Dragon' on their patch? Or was it the demons that had been tricked into thinking Bruce was a girl in his early years finally coming to take him away?

So How Did Bruce Lee Die?

On 10 May 1973, while Bruce was dubbing the sound-track for *Enter the Dragon*, he had a massive seizure and collapsed. His body began convulsing violently and it appeared that he was having an epileptic fit. He was rushed to hospital where Dr Peter Wu diagnosed Bruce as suffering a cerebral oedema. Together with his medical staff Dr Wu managed to bring Bruce around. A small amount of hashish was found in Bruce's stomach and Dr Wu advised him to stop taking it because it could have been the cause of the oedema. Bruce told the doctor that he thought he was making a fuss over nothing and that the hashish was harmless. However, a few weeks later Bruce flew to Los Angeles to have further tests with his own doctor, who could find nothing physically wrong. In fact, he told Bruce that he had the body of an 18-year-old man. Bruce went back to work and continued to push his body to its limit.

On 20 July 1973 Bruce, along with Raymond Chow, went to the house of Betty Ting Pei, a Taiwanese actress whom Bruce had hired to play a role in *Game of Death*. The plan was for the three to discuss the script for the film and then meet actor George Lazenby for dinner. George was also scheduled to star in the film. Shortly afterwards, Raymond left Betty Ting Pei's apartment while Bruce stayed with her to run over the script. At approximately 6:45 pm Bruce complained to Betty that he had a bad headache. She gave him a painkiller, a tablet of equagesic (a compound of meprobomate and aspirin), and Bruce went to lie down on Betty's bed. At approximately 8:10 pm, Betty tried to wake Bruce for their meeting with Raymond Chow and George Lazenby. She panicked when she could not wake him and began to slap his face violently in a bid to revive him. At 9:05 pm, almost an hour after she had first tried to wake Bruce, Betty telephoned Raymond Chow at the bar of the Hotel Miramar where they were scheduled to meet and told him that she could not wake up Bruce. Raymond told Betty not to panic and that he would be over right away. Raymond Chow arrived at Betty's apartment at around 9:40 pm and tried to wake Bruce, but all efforts were in vain. Eventually Betty telephoned her doctor. When Betty's doctor arrived, he immediately called for an ambulance, which rushed Bruce to the Queen Elizabeth Hospital. On the way the paramedics tried to revive Bruce by pounding his chest. The ambulance arrived at the hospital and was met by Bruce's wife Linda. Bruce was rushed into the emergency room, given a stimulant injection and then electric shock treatment to try to restart his heart. Finally, the doctors had to give up and at 9:50 pm, almost two hours after Betty first tried to wake him, Bruce Lee was pronounced dead.

In a press conference organised after Bruce's death, Raymond Chow claimed that Bruce had died peacefully at home and Linda backed up this claim. It was only when the press checked the ambulance records that the truth emerged.

The official verdict was that Bruce's death was a cerebral oedema (swelling of the brain), caused by a hypersensitivity to one or both of the compounds found in the equagesic tablet. His brain had swelled from the normal weight of 1,400 grams to 1,575 grams. The coroner stamped 'Death by Misadventure' on the death certificate.

Bruce had two funeral ceremonies. The first was in a funeral parlour on Maple Street, Hong Kong, where a crowd of over 27,000 people came to pay their last respects. Then on 31 July 1973 Bruce's body was laid to rest at the Lake View cemetery in Seattle, America. The pall-bearers at the funeral included Bruce's friends and students, James Coburn, Steve McQueen, Dan Inosanto and Taky Kimura.

There are some questions worth pondering:

During the flight from Hong Kong to Seattle, Bruce's casket was damaged and blue dye from his suit ran onto the white lining of his coffin. Had someone tampered with the casket? Whatever the reason, the Chinese considered it to be bad luck and claimed that Bruce Lee would never rest in peace.

Why was there so much time between Betty discovering Bruce in a coma at 8:10 pm and his arrival at the hospital at 9:50 pm?

How could Bruce suddenly become hypersensitive to either aspirin or meprobomate when he had previously taken both medicines for his back injury?

Why did Raymond Chow claim that Bruce had died at home and not at the home of Betty Ting Pei?

Apparently Linda Lee never believed the autopsy report on her husband's death, but didn't see the point in delving further because her husband had died and nothing would bring him back. Bruce's son, Brandon, was reportedly going to reopen the inquiry into the death of his father, but sadly he died in 1993 before he had a chance to do so. Since then, Bruce's younger brother Robert has been doing his own research into the death of Bruce Lee and has written a book about the life and death of 'the King of Kung Fu'.

Game of Death (1978)

Cast: Bruce Lee (Billy Lo), Colleen Camp (Ann Morris), Dean Jagger (Dr Land), Gig Young (Jim Marshall), Bob Wall (Carl Miller), Kareem Abdul Jabbar (Hakim), Korean Fighter (Chi Hon Tsoi), Mel Novak (Stick), Hugh O'Brien (Steiner), Dan Inosanto (Pascal)

Crew: Robert Clouse (Director), Raymond Chow (Producer), John Barry (Music)

Notable Stuntmen/Extras: Yuen Biao, Samo Hung

Running Time: 96 mins

Story: The film released posthumously in 1978 bears no resemblance to the original story that Bruce Lee wrote and features only 18 minutes of the man himself. In this version, produced by Raymond Chow, the main character, Billy Lo, is supposedly played by Bruce Lee, but is in fact a combination of doubles, stuntmen and scenes of the real Lee cut from his earlier movies. The basic plot of this outrageous insult to Bruce Lee's memory sees Billy Lo as a famous Kung Fu movie star being leant on by the mob, headed by Dr Land, who want him to join their syndicate. Billy tells the mob he wants no part in it and goes back to work. Whilst shooting a fight scene in the Rome Coliseum (cue extracts from *Way of the Dragon*), a light can falls from the rafters and narrowly missing Billy. It is a warning from the mob and one that gets Billy worried. The syndicate tries to get Billy's signature on the dotted line but Billy once more refuses. This time he won't get away with a warning and whilst filming the finale of his latest film, in which he is to face a firing squad (*Fist of Fury*), he is shot in the face by a real bullet from one of the prop guns. Miraculously Billy survives, but takes the opportunity to fake his own death to escape the mob's threats. (This gives Raymond Chow and Robert

Clouse ample opportunity to use all sorts of disguises and bandages to cover up the face of the actor hired to fill Bruce Lee's shoes.) The mob discover the truth about Billy's fake death and kidnap his girlfriend to get to Billy. Billy arrives at the warehouse where Ann is being held and is ambushed by a motorcycle gang. He easily takes care of the gang and rescues Ann. He takes a motorcycle and one of the bikers' jumpsuits (thus explaining why Bruce is wearing the yellow jumpsuit at the end of the movie) and makes his way to the mob's headquarters.

At this point, we get to see the only real footage of Bruce Lee that he shot for *Game of Death* in 1972. Billy enters Dr Land's lair and immediately comes face to face with Chi Hon Tsoi, one of the martial artists hired to protect the doctor. After getting tossed about the room for a while, Billy rethinks his strategy and soon has the Hap Ki Do Master at his mercy. Eventually lifting him above his head, Billy drops him down onto his outstretched knee, breaking his back. Looking a little bruised and feeling exhausted, Billy makes his way upstairs in search of Dr Land. On the next floor he encounters Hakim, a Master of the Unknown, sitting in a chair wearing dark glasses. Billy can't believe his eyes when he sees Hakim stand at a staggering 7ft 3in tall. Billy quickly runs at Hakim, but Hakim simply outstretches his leg and kicks Billy in the chest, knocking him back several feet. When he gets to his feet again, Billy looks down at his chest and sees a foot-print that stretches from the bottom of his neck right down to his waist. Realising this isn't going to be easy,

Billy steps back to think of a game plan. Hakim stands up out of his chair and Billy looks up at the giant in front of him in awe. Hakim unleashes a flurry of kicks with his long legs, seemingly playing with Billy like a rag doll. One of his kicks sends Billy crashing into a window – light floods through the broken window. (Seems a little strange since Billy entered the building at night-time.) Hakim shields his eyes from the light giving away his secret – he is ultra-sensitive to light. Billy takes advantage of this, quickly attacking Hakim whilst he is struggling to focus his eyes. Soon Billy has Hakim exhausted and with a combination of punches and flying kicks, brings the giant to his knees. He grabs hold of Hakim's neck, chokes the life out of him and finally breaks his neck.

On the next floor, a stand-in for Bruce Lee faces off with Land's right-hand man, 'Stick'. A feeble fight occurs, with Billy leaping and somersaulting his way around the room, like only Bruce Lee wouldn't. Billy kills Stick. Now only Dr Land remains and, realising that Billy has defeated all of his guards, he flees to the roof in a vain attempt to escape. Billy gives chase and just as he is catching up, Dr Land loses his footing and falls from the roof to his death.

Trivia: In one scene you can clearly see a cardboard cut-out of Bruce Lee's face held in front of the double.

Censorship: The complete scene where Bruce fights Dan Inosanto with nunchaku was removed from the UK release of the film – appalling considering that the

actual amount of footage of the real Bruce Lee was
only 18 minutes in total. This cut reduced it to about
12 minutes.

Note: This film has now been released on DVD and
contains all cut scenes.

Verdict: This is a total shambles of a film and an insult
to Bruce Lee's memory. In an interview conducted
some years ago, Raymond Chow said that he couldn't
bear to look at the *Game of Death* footage for a long
time after Bruce's death because it upset him so much
– so much so that Chow sent a camera crew to Bruce's
house the day after he died to film footage for his dire
cash-in documentary *Bruce Lee – The Man and the
Legend*. Chow also included real footage of Bruce Lee
in his casket for the funeral scene of Billy Lo in his
1978 production. Film 2/5 Bruce Lee 3/5
   The fight footage that Bruce shot has been re-edited
so badly for this film that it bears no resemblance to the
original footage. However, fans can now see all of the
footage Bruce shot and in the format he intended
people to see it, thanks to Bruce Lee historian John
Little and the film company which owns the rights to
the footage, Media Asia. Working from Bruce Lee's
original notes, the team painstakingly re-edited the
footage and included it in a documentary that is backed
by Bruce's wife Linda and the Bruce Lee Educational
Foundation. I had the pleasure of viewing this footage
thanks to the charming and very knowledgeable Bey
Logan of Media Asia in 1998, just after it was discov-

ered. I would say that you should watch *Game of Death* for educational purposes, but if you want to see the real footage as Bruce Lee intended, then make sure you get to see *Bruce Lee: A Warrior's Journey.*

The Real Game of Death

Background: When *Game of Death* was released in 1978, it was billed as Bruce Lee's final film and although it did feature Bruce Lee, the film was nothing like the original concept that Bruce had for the film. The 1978 release of the film was basically a rushed project by Raymond Chow and Golden Harvest to capitalise on the ever-growing popularity of Bruce Lee and to satisfy the public demand for the unseen footage Bruce had shot. However, in more recent years, the documentary *Bruce Lee: A Warrior's Journey*, produced by Bruce Lee historian John Little, features all of the original footage that Bruce Lee had filmed for the fight scenes and in the order that he intended it to be viewed. Little painstakingly re-edited the footage, drawing extensively from Bruce Lee's original notes (12 pages of sketches and text), which for years were believed not to exist. For those of you who have viewed the 1978 release of *Game of Death*, let me try to shed some light onto the original story of *Game of Death* and some of the history behind it.

Bruce first had the idea for *Game of Death* in about 1969, but principal shooting did not begin until 1972. Bruce filmed just over one hour of fight footage before he put the project on hold to make *Enter the Dragon.*

Bruce's original script was more than likely a reworking of an idea he had for a film called *The Silent Flute* (see later section), the basic plot being one man's journey to find truth and spiritual enlightenment. *The Silent Flute* evolved from a recurring dream Bruce Lee was having circa 1969. Warner Brothers had already given their backing to the picture, but after James Coburn pulled out of the project the film fell through. After Bruce had become famous in Hong Kong, James Coburn wanted to resurrect *The Silent Flute*, but Bruce was no longer interested – he had moved on and was now shooting *Game of Death*, his dream project.

There have been many rumours as to the original plot of *Game of Death*. It is unlikely we will ever learn the exact details unless the original script for the film resurfaces. In an interview Bruce mentioned how the opening scene would play: a giant tree covered in snow is weathering the winds. All of a sudden, a giant crack is heard and a branch topples from the tree. The camera pans away and we see a tiny willow bending in the wind – it does not break because it has adapted itself to the environment. The lesson Bruce Lee wanted to teach with this scene was that if one is to survive then one must adapt to circumstance.

The plot revolves around a national treasure that has been stolen by an unknown martial arts group and is being kept on an island fortress off Korea. The island is completely guarded by metal detectors so anyone trying to infiltrate the grounds carrying weapons will be immediately sensed. An elite team of fighters led by Bruce Lee's character is sent to the island to try to recover the treasure that is being kept on the top floor of a pagoda. Each floor is guarded by a different Master of the martial arts.

Shortly before Bruce died, George Lazenby (James Bond in *On Her Majesty's Secret Service*) and Betty Ting Pei had agreed to star in *Game of Death*, but which characters they would have played remains a mystery. It is rumoured that Betty Ting Pei was to play Bruce Lee's wife or sister and that either her or their children's kidnapping would be a sub-plot. Lazenby was rumoured to play one of the members of Bruce's team, perhaps an American street fighter, which is believable. The members of the team were as follows:

The Master of Jeet Kune Do: Bruce Lee would play the leader of the group, Hai Tien, an unbeaten martial arts competitor and Master of Jeet Kune Do, the 'style of no style'.

The Master of Kung Fu/Triad gang member: played by James Tien. Tien filmed quite a number scenes for the movie, including fights with Dan Inosanto, Kareem Abdul Jabbar and Chi Hon Tsoi. He is lying dead in the background of the 1978 release when Bruce fights Jabbar.

The Master of Karate: played by Chieh Yuan. Again Chieh shot footage for the film including fights with Inosanto and Chi Hon Tsoi.

A fighter, perhaps an American Karate expert: possibly to be played by Chuck Norris or Bob Wall. This character was only a rumour so no footage exists.

A fighter, perhaps an American street fighter: possibly George Lazenby's character. Again, no footage exists because Bruce died before Lazenby began work on the film.

Lock pick: Not a lot is known about this character except that he was a lock pick and would be essential in order for the team to gain entrance to the pagoda.

As for the Masters of the pagoda, again the information is a little sketchy but it is possible that this is how the set-up may have been planned:

Outside entrance: a team of ten Karate-ka. There was also a rumour that the outside was guarded by a hulking character, possibly played by Bolo Yeung (Yang Tze). Rumours have been around for many years that stills of Bruce fighting the giant exist and that he is not played by Bolo. However, footage of Whang In Sik fighting with the ten Karate-ka was shot so this is the most likely theory.

First Floor: the high-kicking Whang In Sik from *Way of the Dragon* would guard this floor. No footage was ever shot of this floor.

Second Floor: the Hall of the Mantis. The character in this sequence was to be played by Bruce Lee's good friend Taky Kimura – he was one of only three people that Bruce Lee had certified in Jeet Kune Do. Taky was to play a Master of Praying Mantis Kung Fu, but was unable to fly out for filming due to a death in the family. This scene was never shot. Taky had received a plane ticket from Bruce and was due to fly out to Hong Kong just days before Bruce died.

Third Floor: the Hall of the Tiger. This scene was

filmed. Dan Inosanto played the Tiger in the film and his scenes with Bruce are probably the most exciting of those actually shot. Bruce fights with a bamboo cane and nunchaku, whilst Dan fights with Escrima sticks and nunchaku. This scene appears in all international prints of the 1978 release, but with the original footage heavily edited.

Fourth Floor: the Hall of the Dragon. This scene was filmed. The character on this floor is a Master of Hap Ki Do and is played by Chi Hon Tsoi. This scene appears in all international prints of the 1978 release, but with the original footage heavily edited.

Fifth Floor: the Hall of the Unknown. This scene was filmed. The master on the final floor is the Master of the Unknown, a giant of a man whose fighting style is unorthodox. LA Lakers basketball star and Bruce Lee student Kareem Abdul Jabbar plays the character guarding this level of the pagoda. This scene appears in all prints of the 1978 release, but with the original footage heavily edited.

Story: Hai Tien is travelling home on an aeroplane with his sister and little brother when the flight has to make a temporary stop at a Korean airport. He leaves his sister and brother in the waiting lounge to take a telephone call. The voice on the other end of the tele-phone tells him that they have his sister and brother, but they won't be harmed as long as he complies. Hai Tien is taken by car to the home of a Korean mob boss who wants him and five hired fighters to go to a pagoda and steal a national treasure that is being kept there. Hai

Tien is offered money but declines – he must still complete the mission to save his brother and sister.

The team arrives on the island and observes a group of martial artists training outside the pagoda. (Dan Inosanto said that this sequence was shot in the New Territories of Hong Kong, but the film is missing.) On the way to the pagoda the group is faced by the Karate-ka. A mass battle erupts and, after a long and tiring fight, the team destroy all the guards. The lock pick unlocks the door to the pagoda then keeps guard as the five fighters enter.

Inside the pagoda the team comes face to face with Whang In Sik. Bruce Lee's notes do not say which fighter defeats Whang and no footage was shot. However, one of the team, possibly the American Karate expert, loses his life to Whang.

The remaining four fighters go up to the next level, where they are greeted by the Master of Praying Mantis Kung Fu. The American street fighter makes a move on the Mantis fighter but is soon defeated. The Karate Master attacks the Mantis Master with a wooden staff. Eventually the Master of Praying Mantis is killed, but we do not know by whom because the scene was not filmed.

The fighters make their way up to the next level of the pagoda. James Tien's character, carrying a club, is no match for the Escrima-wielding Tiger, played by Dan Inosanto, and is soon left in an aching heap on the floor. Chieh Yuan arrives and suffers a similar fate at the claws of the Tiger. Hai Tien arrives, strikes at the Tiger with his bamboo cane and pulls his companion to safety. A long and tactical fight ensues with nunchaku. The Tiger becomes so frustrated by Hai Tien that he can no longer fight effectively. James Tien and Chieh Yuan watch on in amazement as Hai Tien disarms the Tiger and, in a final flurry of strikes and kicks, wraps his nunchaku round his neck and strangles him.

On the next floor, the three fighters see Chi Hon Tsoi reclining on a couch. Chieh Yuan attacks first but cannot land a single blow on Tsoi, a Master of Hap Ki Do. James Tien joins in the attack, but both fighters are easily countered. Meanwhile Hai Tien watches from the sidelines, taking mental notes of Tsoi's style of fighting. After a few more futile attacks at Tsoi, Hai Tien pulls his companions out of danger and steps forward to face Tsoi himself. The Korean makes a move on him, but is stopped in his tracks by a powerful kick to the head. Hai Tien begins dancing around his opponent, moving in and out of range and constantly circling him. Tsoi is puzzled and doesn't know what to do, whilst Hai Tien strikes at will. Hai Tien allows himself to be grabbed by Tsoi, but each time this happens, he delivers a number of crushing blows to the body.

Chieh Yuan takes the opportunity to dash up to the next level but, to Hai Tien's disbelief, Chieh Yuan's lifeless body soon comes crashing back down the stairs. James Tien, in a state of rage, makes his way up the stairs seeking revenge, where he sees the Master of the Unknown, a giant of a man standing at 7ft 3in and played by Kareem Abdul Jabbar. A terrified Tien runs up to the final floor where the lost treasure is stored in a chest but, just as he gets near the top, the giant Jabbar reaches up the stairs and pulls Tien back down over the handrail. Jabbar grabs hold of Tien round the neck and tosses him across the room. Downstairs, Hai Tien raises Tsoi above his head and brings him down on his outstretched knee, breaking Tsoi's back.

A weary Hai Tien hears a cry of pain from upstairs and, as he rushes up, he has to duck as James Tien's body goes hurtling past. Upstairs, the room is dark and it takes a while for Hai Tien's eyes to adjust but when they do, he is awestruck by the sight of the giant in front of him wearing shorts and a pair of sunglasses. The two fight, with Hai Tien being repelled at each attack. As Jabbar sends Hai Tien sprawling backwards into the paper window of the pagoda, the window breaks and sunlight floods into the room, causing Jabbar to shield his face. Hai Tien realises the big man is affected by light, so he punches out all the windows to allow the light to stream in. With Jabbar temporarily blinded, Hai Tien attacks with a barrage of head butts, punches, kicks and groin strikes. Finally, with a magnificent leaping kick to the head, Hai Tien brings the giant down, removing his glasses in the process – the giant has eyes like a lizard caused by a rare condition known as photosensitivity. As Jabbar searches for his shades, Hai Tien asks, 'Why continue? Why don't you just let me pass?' 'Have you forgotten that I am not afraid of death?' replies Jabbar. With that, Hai Tien continues his onslaught, grabs hold of Jabbar round the neck and keeps on squeezing until finally the life is drained out of his mighty foe.

Hai Tien rises, physically and emotionally exhausted, then makes his way upstairs to retrieve the treasure. It has never been known exactly what the treasure was going to be, but there are a couple of rumours and both seem feasible. The first is that the treasure is a mirror. This is highly likely, as this idea was used in *The Silent Flute*, which was the starting point for *Game of Death*. The second possibility is that the treasure was a piece of paper containing the words: 'Life is but a process of waiting for death.' I personally favour the mirror explanation.

The final scene sees Hai Tien walk down the stairs and pause at the window where there is an exchange of dialogue between him and somebody outside. It is assumed the conversation is with the lock pick:

Hai Tien: Come on up!
Lock Pick: Is it safe?
Hai Tien: Yes.
Lock Pick: Your job is done, come on down.
Hai Tien moves down a level then shouts again.
Hai Tien: Help me!
Lock Pick: Hurry down.
The film fades out.

Verdict: The full storyline is not known because nobody has seen a complete script. Raymond Chow claimed that a script never existed and that only Bruce knew the exact story details. Yet he also said that on the day he died Bruce was at Betty Ting Pei's apartment going over the script. Both Ting Pei and George

Lazenby had apparently seen the script and since George was an actor of slightly higher calibre than any of the other stars of the film, it is unlikely he would have agreed to sign up for a film that didn't even have a script. It is also worth mentioning that in some of the out-takes for the fight sequences Bruce is clearly seen holding a clapperboard with the scene and take number on. Why would anybody bother having a scene number on a clapperboard if they didn't have a script to which to link it?

The Legend Lives On

The Silent Flute (1979)

Cast: David Carradine (The Blind Man, Monkeyman, Death, Chang Sha), Christopher Lee (Zetan), Jeff Cooper (Cord), Roddy McDowell (White Robe), Anthony DeLongis (Morthond), Earl Maynard (Black Giant), Erica Creer (Tanya), Eli Wallach (Man in Oil)

Running Time: 102 mins

Although Bruce never appeared in this film, in my opinion he had enough input into it for it to be included in this book.

Story: The story follows a martial artist named Cord on his quest to find truth in the Book of All Knowledge possessed by a grand wizard named Zetan. After entering a tournament to win the right to seek the wizard, Cord is disqualified and another martial artist is awarded the right to go on the quest. Cord believes that he should be the one going, so follows the chosen one. On his travels the chosen one must overcome many challenges to get the Book. However, the chosen one is killed at his first challenge, so Cord takes his place as the rightful seeker of the truth. At appropriate moments on Cord's journey a flute player appears and helps guide Cord through his trials. Eventually Cord gets to the kingdom of Zetan and wins the right to see the Book of All Knowledge. Opening the book, he is aghast to see that every page is... a mirror, illustrating that the truth is inside us.

Background: Bruce Lee first had the idea for *The Silent Flute* in 1969 from a series of recurring dreams about a seeker of truth. The dreams were probably reflections of his own life. Bruce had intended to shoot the film in 1969 with James Coburn and Sterling Silliphant. Warner Brothers had already agreed to the movie on the condition that it would be shot on location in India, where they had a lot of frozen assets. Location scouting began in 1971, when Bruce, Coburn and Silliphant headed off to India. The journey was very tiring and was looking futile. Coburn and Silliphant both agreed that they couldn't find a location in India and thought it best if they headed home. For Bruce Lee though, this wasn't just about making his film, it was about making his career and being able to support his family – he had to get the film made. Eventually he persuaded his two partners to continue their search for a location and the three of them boarded a plane for Madras and then on to Goa. They still had no luck. The trip seemed more and more pointless and the tensions were becoming unbearable. They left Goa for Bombay and checked into the Taj

Mahal Hotel. James Coburn received the biggest room in the hotel, bigger than the dining area, while Bruce's room was little bigger than a broom cupboard. That was a tremendous blow to Bruce's ego and that night he vowed he would be bigger than both James Coburn and another of his famous students, Steve McQueen. The three left Bombay for California, totally dejected. Warner Brothers had only agreed to fund the project if it was shot in India and there was no way James Coburn was going to film in that country – he was accustomed to the star treatment afforded to Hollywood celebrities and he wasn't going to get it in India. Coburn pulled out of the project and along with him went the backing from Warner Brothers. For Bruce Lee, this felt like the end of the world. How would he support his family now?

Trivia: Bruce Lee first approached Steve McQueen to play the role of Cord in the movie, but McQueen said he was too busy. When Bruce persisted in asking McQueen to star, the real reason for him not accepting became apparent. McQueen said, 'Be honest. This is a film to make Bruce Lee into a star. I like you but I'm not here to make you a star. I'm not going to carry you on my back.' This enraged Bruce and as he left McQueen's house he turned to Sterling Silliphant and, shaking his fist back at McQueen's house, said, 'I'm going to be bigger than he is.'

Verdict: It is hard to imagine how the film may have turned out if Bruce Lee would have made it; one thing is for sure, David Carradine would have had no part in it. The wooden acting and dire martial arts skills from both leads detract from what could have possibly been a classic film. The storyline is very good, but how it compares to the original idea Bruce Lee had remains unknown. Film 3/5

Dragon: The Bruce Lee Story (1993)

Cast: Jason Scott Lee (Bruce Lee), Lauren Holly (Linda Lee), Robert Wagner (Bill Krieger), Michael Learned (Vivian Emery), Nancy Kwan (Gussie Yang)

Crew: Rob Cohen (Director)

Notable Stuntmen/Extras: Shannon Lee

Running Time: 107 mins

Story: Based on Linda Lee's 1989 biography of her late husband, *Dragon* supposedly tells the true story of Bruce Lee's life. The film is heavily flawed with inaccuracies and Hollywood glamorisation. Jason Scott Lee (no relation) is very convincing in the title role, but the film is let down by the fictional elements used to increase the drama. It is a great shame that the producers felt it necessary to over-dramatise what is a dramatic story in its own right. A good example is the back injury that Bruce received. In the film he injures his back during a fight with Wong Jack Man – in real life Bruce damaged his back whilst lifting weights without warming up.

Trivia: Linda Lee wanted to make a biography of her husband in the mid-1970s and even went as far as casting gymnast Alex Kwon as Bruce.

Verdict: As an action film *Dragon* is quite a good romp. As a Bruce Lee biography the film is flawed and inaccurate. If you want to know and understand Bruce Lee you would be better reading a good book on the subject. This one perhaps. Film 3/5 Jason Scott Lee 5/5

Bruceploitation

Since Bruce Lee's death there have been countless imitators all billed to be the new King of Kung Fu. Among these were Dragon Lee, Bruce Le, Bruce Lo, Bruce Lia and even Bluce Ree. But by far the most successful was Ho Chung Tao, better known as Bruce Li. Ho Chung Tao was a physical education teacher specialising in gymnastics at a Taiwan high school in 1974 when a talent scout noticed a vague resemblance to Bruce Lee. He was quickly signed up for one of the first Bruce Lee rip-off pictures, *Dragon Dies Hard*, a supernatural thriller that had Ho Chung Tao visited by the ghost of Bruce Lee, who tells him that foul play was involved in his death and that Ho Chung Tao must investigate and bring the culprits to justice. All very sleazy if you ask me! Anyway, the film made quite an impact and spurred a host of similar Bruce Lee rip-offs starring Ho Chung Tao, who now objected to being known as Bruce Li and wanted to be billed under his real name. The producers usually agreed to this just to keep Ho happy, but invariably upon the film's release the star would be billed as 'Bruce Li' and the film title would be changed to include a reference to Bruce Lee – for example, *Bruce Lee Against Supermen*, *Bruce Against Iron Hand* and *Bruce Lee in New Guinea*. Most of these were complete rubbish and had nothing to do with the real Bruce Lee. However, Ho Chung Tao did make one film which I think is worth including in this book, *Bruce Lee, The Man, The Myth*, which was a biography of the life and death of Bruce Lee. In my opinion, it is more realistic than *Dragon*.

Bruce Lee, The Man, The Myth (1976)

Cast: Ho Chung Tao (credited as 'Bruce Li', plays Bruce Lee), Caryn White (Linda Lee), Unicorn Chan (Himself)
Director: Ng See Yuen

Running Time: 70 mins

Story: The film traces Bruce's life from his beginnings in Hong Kong to his trip to America, where he made *The Green Hornet*, and back to Hong Kong to make motion pictures. It is not 100 per cent accurate, but is less far-fetched than the Hollywood production. Ho Chung Tao worked hard for this role and his preparation shows. He really gives his all in his portrayal of Bruce Lee, and the fight scenes, although nowhere near the standard of Bruce Lee's, are a lot more realistic than in any of Ho Chung Tao's previous films. The film contains actual footage from Bruce Lee's funeral in Hong Kong, but what makes this film stand out from the others is that it offers three versions of Bruce Lee's death: the official verdict, which sees Bruce take a painkiller at the home of Betty Ting Pei; a gang of sword-wielding gangsters killing Bruce; and Bruce going into hiding for ten years planning to return in 1983 (I think he is a bit late for that one).

Verdict: If you want to see a more truthful account of Bruce Lee's life than the story offered in *Dragon*, then this film is for you. Film 3/5 Ho Chung Tao 3/5

Whilst on the subject of exploitation, it is worth mentioning a film made in 1972 that had the nerve to exploit Bruce whilst he was still alive. The film in question was called *Fists of the Unicorn*, which was basically a starring vehicle for Bruce's childhood friend Unicorn Chan. The film's producer had offered Unicorn the role on the proviso that he could get Bruce involved. Unicorn approached Bruce fully expecting him to refuse, but to his surprise Bruce agreed to help his old friend out, even though he knew he was being exploited. However, not even Bruce knew the full extent to which he would be exploited. The film began shooting in August 1972 and Bruce spent a full day on set directing the fight action and also adding scenes to the script to try to save the picture from certain doom.

When the film was released shortly afterwards, Bruce was shocked to see that he was given star billing on all the posters and press releases as the lead actor. Footage of Bruce attending a press conference for the film and also footage of him on set giving directions had been cut into the finished film and the story had been changed to reflect the changes. Needless to say, Bruce was furious with Unicorn and issued a legal letter disassociating himself from the project.

I will also briefly mention the awful *Game of Death 2* in this section, as it is simply further exploitation. It basically contains a few out-takes from *Enter the Dragon* and little more. It is so bad that it doesn't deserve any more coverage; I did say it would be brief.

Documentaries

Bruce Lee – The Man and the Legend (1973)

Producer: Raymond Chow

Running Time: 94 mins

Synopsis: Produced by Raymond Chow literally days after Bruce Lee's death in Hong Kong, this documentary was dubbed by Chow as a tribute to his friend Bruce. The film contains footage of Bruce's funerals in Hong Kong and Seattle, and also has footage of the removal men packing up Bruce's belongings in his home in Kowloon. This doesn't seem like much of a tribute to me. On the plus side, the documentary contains rare footage of Bruce Lee's final film *Game of Death*, and also a plethora of rare photographs. However, with the release of Bruce's films uncut on DVD, the only reason to buy this video would be for the rare photographs. This is a poor excuse to cash in on Bruce Lee's name and leaves a bad taste in your mouth.

Bruce Lee – The Legend (1983)

Producer: Raymond Chow

Running Time: 90 mins

Synopsis: Raymond Chow's second attempt to cash in on Bruce Lee, this time in 1983. A better production than the rushed 1973 documentary, it is a good introduction to new fans wanting to learn about Bruce Lee. It offers clips from all of Bruce's films plus some rare television footage and unseen footage from *Game of Death*.

Bruce Lee – Martial Arts Master (1993)

Producer: Gary Shoefield

Running Time: 70 mins

Synopsis: A good telling of the life and death of Bruce Lee, but offers little in the way of rare footage and new information.

Death by Misadventure (1994)

Director: Toby Russell

Running Time: 91 mins

Synopsis: Some excellent rare footage and in-depth information concerning Bruce Lee's death make this a fascinating video. Also includes an exclusive interview with Bruce's son Brandon.

Bruce Lee – Jeet Kune Do (1995)

Director: Walt Missingham

Running Time: 56 mins

Synopsis: Using recordings from Bruce Lee's private audio files and interviews, Walt Missingham presents what could be described as the only Jeet Kune Do training tape featuring Bruce Lee. Although this is not a how-to demonstration, it does give the viewer the best insight possible into Bruce Lee's personal martial arts training. The film features lots of rarely seen footage of Bruce Lee teaching James Coburn in his garden, plus footage from most of his movies and clips from the only available interview Bruce Lee gave in Hong Kong. Also featured is an interview and demonstration of Jeet Kune Do by Bruce's top student, Dan Inosanto. All this with Bruce Lee's own narration make *Jeet Kune Do* a must-have for anyone interested in the King of Kung Fu.

Intercepting Fist (1998)

Director: Walt Missingham

Running Time: 55 mins

Synopsis: The second release from Walt Missingham brings to light some really rare footage from Bruce Lee's uncompleted *Game of Death*.

The Path of the Dragon (2000)

Director: Walt Missingham

Running Time: 60 mins

Synopsis: A thorough examination into the life and legend of Bruce Lee. Once again, Missingham does a great job of bringing lots of archive footage to this presentation. Also has the added bonus of being narrated by Bruce Lee's daughter Shannon.

Reference Materials

Books

There have been many books written about Bruce Lee, his art, his philosophy and his films. Some are by Bruce Lee himself, others are by his original students, while others by writers like myself, who either have a keen interest in martial art or just in Bruce Lee. Of all the current books on the market by far the most insightful are the recent publications from Tuttle. These are sanctioned by the Bruce Lee Educational Foundation and edited by John Little, probably the only person in the world to have been given access to all of Bruce Lee's personal notes, writings, diaries and personal possessions

Written by Bruce Lee
The Tao of Jeet Kune Do by Bruce Lee, December 1975, O'Hara Publications, paperback, 208 pages, ISBN 0897500482

This is often falsely claimed to be a training manual by Bruce Lee, when in fact it is made up of notes and sketches that Bruce wrote whilst he was in bed with a back injury. It was released posthumously in 1975.

Chinese Kung Fu – The Philosophical Art of Self Defence by Bruce Lee, February 1997 (3rd Edition), O'Hara Publications, paperback, 97 pages, ISBN 0897501128

Originally published in 1964, this book is basically a collection of pictures of Wing Chun techniques for self-defence applications. The pictures are of rather low quality and the text is minimal, but it is still a great historical insight into the martial art Bruce Lee was practising before he developed Jeet Kune Do.

Jeet Kune Do by Bruce Lee, edited by John Little, November 1997, Tuttle Publishing, paperback, 399 pages, ISBN 0804831327

Billed as a sequel to *The Tao of Jeet Kune Do*, John Little edits more of Bruce Lee's original notes. Packed with Bruce's philosophy, training methods and original sketches, this book is an absolute must for all those interested in Jeet Kune Do.

Words From a Master by Bruce Lee, edited by John Little, November 1998, Contemporary Books, hardback, 128 pages, ISBN 0809228564

A collection of interviews with Bruce Lee that reveals his personal philosophy and thoughts on such issues as racism, success and the challenge and triumphs of his personal and professional life.

The Art of Expressing the Human Body by Bruce Lee,

edited by John Little, December 1998, Charles E. Tuttle, paperback, 256 pages, ISBN 0804831297

Drawing on Lee's notes, letters, diaries and training logs, bodybuilding expert John Little presents Bruce Lee's fitness techniques.

Letters of the Dragon by Bruce Lee, edited by John Little, December 1998, Tuttle Publishing, paperback, 256 pages, ISBN 0804831114

A collection of Bruce Lee's personal and business correspondence shows Bruce to be a kind, warm, optimistic and loyal man.

Striking Thoughts by Bruce Lee, edited by John Little, April 2000, Tuttle Publishing, paperback, 239 pages, ISBN 0804832218

A collection of thoughts and writings from Bruce Lee. This is essential reading.

About Bruce Lee

The Making of Enter the Dragon by Robert Clouse, June 1987, Unique Publications, paperback, 206 pages, ISBN 0865680698

A book from the director of *Enter the Dragon*. Clouse concentrates on the production of the world's best-known martial arts film. Packed with tons of photographs, both on and off set, and insightful background information, this book deserves repeated readings.

The Bruce Lee Story by Linda Lee, April 1989, O'Hara Publications, paperback, 100 pages, ISBN 0897501217

Bruce Lee's widow traces his life from his childhood in Hong Kong to his education in the United States, his career as an actor and his untimely death. The book was originally a collaboration between Linda and her second husband Tom Bleecker, author of *Unsettled Matters*. However, after their divorce Linda had Bleecker's name removed from all subsequent pressings.

Unsettled Matters by Tom Bleecker, July 1996, Gilderoy Publishing, paperback, ISBN 0965313204

Without a doubt the most controversial book written about Bruce Lee. Tom Bleecker was a friend and student of Bruce and was also married to his widow, Linda. This book is a shocking tale of drugs use, steroid abuse, tantrums and murder. Tom Bleecker leaves no stone unturned in this warts and all biography, which many believe to be totally inaccurate. Well worth a read for those who aren't easily shocked and upset.

Fighting Spirit by Bruce Thomas, February 1997, Pan Publishing, paperback, 384 pages, ISBN 0330349309

This biography examines not only Bruce's life, but also the philosophy and fighting skills that made him the icon he is.

Bruce Lee: The Biography by Robert Clouse, August 1998, Unique Publications, paperback, 194 pages, ISBN 0865681333

A biography of Bruce Lee by the director of *Enter the Dragon*. Not the most detailed of biographies, but still a good read. An excellent selection of pictures makes up for what the book lacks in editorial content.

Intercepting Fist – The Films of Bruce Lee by Jack Hunter, November 1999, Glitter Books, paperback, ISBN 1902588053

Jack Hunter edits a collection of film reviews and reports by fans of Bruce Lee. The book covers all five of Bruce Lee's films, from *The Big Boss* through to *Game of Death*.

The Tao of Bruce Lee by Davis Miller, 2000, Vintage, paperback, 177 pages, ISBN 009977951

Davis Miller combines a biography of Bruce Lee with his own experiences growing up in North Carolina. A fascinating read that keeps you on the edge of your seat, as much to discover the future for Miller as for Bruce Lee.

DVDs

All of the following DVDs are currently available in the UK from most video shops or from amazon.co.uk. I have only included those DVDs that in my opinion have some worth to the Bruce Lee fan.

DVDs Available
Watching the Detectives Volume 1 Includes Bruce Lee in the *Ironside* episode (2000)
The Path of the Dragon (2000)
The Unbeatable Bruce Lee (2001)

Game of Death (2001)
Bruce Lee – A Warrior's Journey (2001)
Death by Misadventure (2003)
Bruce Lee – The Intercepting Fist (2003)
Bruce Lee – The Man, the Legend (2003)
Way of the Dragon – Platinum Edition (2003)
The Real Bruce Lee (2003)
Bruce Lee – Jeet Kune Do (2003)
Enter the Dragon – Special Edition (2004)
Bruce Lee Interviews with the Master (2004)
Fury of the Dragon – Bruce Lee in The Green Hornet
(2004)
The Big Boss – Two Disc Platinum Edition
(2006)
Fist of Fury (2006)
Bruce Lee – The Immortal Dragon (2007)
Bruce Lee – Martial Arts Master (2007)
The Kid (2007)
Bruce Lee – The Early Years 1953/1955 (2008)

Websites

There are literally thousands of websites devoted to Bruce Lee and to list them all would take a book in itself, so I have listed some of the more interesting sites, many of which have links to other sites.

My Tribute to Bruce Lee –
http://www.siuloong.co.uk – come and join the community to discuss all things Bruce Lee.

Bruce Lee Fan Club UK –
http://www.brucelee.org.uk/ – A UK-based fan site with lots of information, reviews and an online store.

Bruce Lee Educational Foundation –
http://www.jkd.com/ – The official site of the Jun Fan Jeet Kune Do Nucleus, headed by Bruce's widow, Linda Lee Cadwell.

Bruce Lee Timeline

1940

- 27 November, Bruce Lee is born in the Year of the Dragon between 6:00 am and 8:00 am, the Hour of the Dragon, at the Jackson Street Hospital in San Francisco's Chinatown. His father and mother were travelling the US whilst touring with the Cantonese Opera troupe with which Lee Hoi Chuen, Bruce's father, was performing.
- At three months old, Bruce debuts in the film *Golden Gate Girl* in San Francisco. He plays a female baby, carried by his father.

1941

- Bruce and his parents return to Kowloon, Hong Kong. They move into an apartment at 218 Nathan Road, Kowloon district.

1946

- Makes his first major childhood movie *The Birth of Mankind*. Later this year he appears in *My Son Ah Cheung*. Bruce goes on to appear in over a dozen more films in Hong Kong. In these films, he is usually cast as a street urchin.

- Becomes near-sighted and starts wearing glasses. (He will later wear contacts, as suggested to him by an optometrist friend.)

1952
- Begins attending La Salle College.

1953
- Takes up Wing Chun Kung Fu under Grandmaster Yip Man.

1954
- Starts cha-cha dancing and also joins the street gang, 'the Junction Street 8 Tigers'.

1957
- Enters an amateur boxing tournament whilst attending St Francis Xavier High School and defeats the champion of the three previous years.

1958
- Wins the Crown Colony cha-cha championship.
- Has a leading role in the film *The Orphan* as a James Dean-type rebel. This is the last movie Bruce makes as a child actor and, interestingly, the only film in which he doesn't fight.

1959
- Gets into numerous street fights whilst in Hong Kong and gets into trouble with the police. On his father's suggestion it is decided that Bruce will return

to America before his eighteenth birthday to gain his
American citizenship.

1959
- Arrives in San Francisco with $100, then moves on
  to Seattle. Here he lives at a Chinese restaurant
  owned by Ruby Chow, a friend of his father. He lives
  in a room above the restaurant whilst working as a
  waiter downstairs.
- Enrols in Edison Technical College and gains his
  high-school diploma.
- Teaches Wing Chun to his friends in backyards and
  city parks.

1961
- Enrols at the University of Washington, majoring in
  Philosophy.
- Begins teaching Kung Fu to students at school.

1963
- Returns to Hong Kong with friend Doug Palmer to
  visit his family for the first time since his arrival in
  the US.
- Returns to Seattle at the end of the summer to
  continue his education.
- Gives talks on philosophy at Garfield High School
  where he catches the eye of Linda Emery.
- Moves out of Ruby Chow's restaurant and opens his
  first Kung Fu school.

1964

- Meets Tae Kwon Do teacher Jhoon Rhee and Dan Inosanto at the Long Beach International Karate Tournament. Jay Sebring, the hairstylist for *Batman* producer William Dozier, spots him. Sebring gives Dozier a copy of the film he shot of Bruce; Dozier plans to use Bruce in a new production, a spin-off of the Charlie Chan series called *Number One Son*.
- Makes plans with James Yimm Lee to open a second Jun Fan Kung Fu Institute in Oakland, CA. His good friend, Taky Kimura, takes over as head instructor.
- Returns to Seattle to marry Linda. They soon move to Oakland.
- Flies to Los Angeles for a screen test for *Number One Son*.

1965

- Challenged by Wong Jack Man, a leading Kung Fu practitioner in the Chinatown Community, for teaching his Kung Fu to Westerners. They agree that if Bruce loses, he will either close his school, or stop teaching Caucasians; or if Jack loses, he will stop teaching. Bruce defeats Wong. However, he realises that the fight took longer than he had anticipated and has to re-evaluate his system of fighting. From this encounter Jeet Kune Do was born.
- *Number One Son* fails to see the light of day. However, William Dozier has another show in the pipeline and Bruce is signed up for a one-year contract to play Kato in *The Green Hornet*.
- Bruce and Linda's first child Brandon Bruce Lee is

born on 1 February.

- Returns to Hong Kong for his father's funeral. As tradition dictates, in order to obtain forgiveness for not being present when his father died, Bruce crawls on his knees across the floor of the funeral home towards the casket, wailing loudly and crying.

- Uses the first cheque from *The Green Hornet* to fly himself, Linda and Brandon back to Hong Kong to settle his father's estate. While in Hong Kong, Bruce takes Brandon to see Yip Man, to persuade Yip to perform on tape. Bruce wants to take the footage back to Seattle and show his students what the man looks like in action. Yip modestly declines.

1966

- Filming begins on *The Green Hornet*, for which Bruce is paid $400 per episode. Bruce suggested he got the part because he was the only Oriental person they could find who could accurately pronounce the name Britt Reid.

1967

- Opens his third school at 628 College Street, Los Angeles, CA. Dan Inosanto becomes Bruce's assistant instructor.

- The last episode of *The Green Hornet* is aired on 24 March 1967.

- Is the special guest star in the *Ironside* episode, *Tagged For Murder*.

- Charges up to $250 an hour for private tuition to celebrities such as Steve McQueen and James Coburn.

1968
- Appears in the television shows *Blondie* and *Here Come the Brides*.

1969
- Plays Winslow Wong in *Marlowe*.
- Bruce and Linda's second child Shannon is born on 19 April.
- Bruce, Sterling Silliphant and James Coburn begin work on a script for *The Silent Flute*.

1970
- Injures his sacral nerve and experiences severe muscle spasms in his back whilst training. Doctors tell him that he will never practise martial arts again. During the months of recovery he starts to document his training methods and his philosophy of Jeet Kune Do.
- Bruce and Brandon fly to Hong Kong and are welcomed by fans of *The Green Hornet*.
- Bruce sends his friend Unicorn Chan to talk to Run Run Shaw on his behalf and informs Shaw that he would be willing to do a movie for him for $10,000. Shaw makes a counter-offer of a seven-year contract and $2,000 per film (the standard junior actors' contract). Bruce declines.

1971
- Bruce, James Coburn and Sterling Silliphant fly to India to scout locations for *The Silent Flute*. They spend one month searching, but are forced to call off the search because Coburn backs out of the project.

This trip gives Bruce the idea for *Game of Death*.

- Takes a short trip back to Hong Kong to arrange for his mother to live in the US. He is shocked to discover that airings of *The Green Hornet* have made him a national hero and he makes an appearance on one of the most popular TV shows in Hong Kong. Later, he is approached by Raymond Chow of Golden Harvest and offered the lead role in a new film called *The Big Boss*. Bruce accepts.

- Is supplied with an apartment at 2 Man Wan Road, Kowloon, Hong Kong. Brandon attends La Salle College, the same school Bruce attended only 15 years before.

- Interviewed by Canadian talk show host, Pierre Berton, and speaks candidly about his philosophy and martial arts. This is the only available television interview of Bruce in existence.

- Filming begins for *The Big Boss* (released in the US as *Fists of Fury*). It breaks all box-office records.

- Bruce receives a telegram, notifying him that he has not been chosen for the part in the upcoming series *The Warrior*. This series was later released as *Kung Fu*, staring David Carradine.

1972

- *Fist of Fury* (released in the US as *The Chinese Connection*) is released. It breaks all the previous records set by *The Big Boss*.

- Appears on Hong Kong's TVB channel for a hurricane disaster relief benefit. In a demo Bruce breaks four out of five boards. Brandon even breaks a board with a side kick!

- Helps his friend Unicorn Chan by choreographing the fight scenes for the film *Fists of the Unicorn*. Bruce is shocked to discover that footage of him on set appears in the final release and that his name has received star billing.
- Third film is *Way of the Dragon* (released in the US as *The Return of the Dragon*). This time Bruce gets almost complete control over the movie. He writes, directs, choreographs and stars.
- Begins work on *Game of Death* and films several fight scenes with Danny Inosanto, Kareem Abdul Jabbar and Chi Hon Tsoi.
- During shooting of *Game of Death*, Bruce gets an offer from Warner Brothers to star in an American-made martial arts film, *Enter the Dragon*. Work on *Game of Death* is halted.

1973

- Bruce tells film director Robert Clouse's wife that he doubts he will live long enough to see his next birthday.
- On 10 May Bruce is at Golden Harvest Studios in Hong Kong dubbing his voice for *Enter the Dragon* when he collapses. He is rushed to hospital where Dr Peter Wu revives him. He has suffered a cerebral oedema (swelling of the brain).
- On 20 July 1973 Bruce Lee dies at the home of film star Betty Ting Pei. The official cause is cerebral oedema caused by hypersensitivity to a painkiller. Verdict: Death by Misadventure.

Index